The Prayer
~ Trilogy ~

Peter's Prayer

By
Jared T. Bigham

Tate Publishing, LLC

Published in the United States of America
By TATE PUBLISHING, LLC
All rights reserved.
Do not duplicate without permission.

All Scripture references are King James Version,
unless otherwise indicated.

Book Design by TATE PUBLISHING, LLC.

Printed in the United States of America by
TATE PUBLISHING, LLC
127 East Trade Center Terrace
Mustang, OK 73064
(888) 361-9473

Publisher's Cataloging in Publication

Bigham, Jared

Peter's Prayer / Jared Bigham

Originally published in Mustang,OK:TATE PUBLISHING:2004

1. Youth / Christian Fiction 2. Adventure / Archaeology

ISBN 1-9331484-8-9 $14.95

Copyright 2005

First Printing: January 2005

Dedication

For Albie and Calvin.
Thank you for your love and support.

Prologue

67 A.D. Tullian Keep, Rome

The man sat down on the floor and laid his head of matted, dirty hair against the pillar he had been chained to for the past nine months. The only sounds to be heard in the dark and musty cell were the rats that scurried in and out of holes that led to other cells and passageways. Even the rats didn't seem to want to stay long in the fetid cell.

The man's mind wandered to places and senses far away. He recalled images of emerald green waters and the sensation of a gently rocking boat in a salty breeze. The man had once been a fisherman, and he loved the sea. But his memories did not bring sadness. They were just one of the ways he found to pass the time. Other than praying and talking to a guard now and then, reminiscing was the only other thing to do in the empty cell.

Talking to a guard was becoming a less frequent activity because of the man's influence on them—for the man was a Christian, an agitator and menace with with dissentious beliefs in the eyes of Rome, and he had converted almost every guard who came in contact with him to his dissentious beliefs. For this reason, guards were now only allowed minimum contact with this prisoner.

The man stretched his legs in front of him and stared at the bare wall that he could vaguely make out in the darkness. It was then he sensed a presence in the room. He stood up and looked around. To his left, in the darkest corner of the cell, there seemed to be someone standing there, but it was too dark for the man to be sure.

"Hello? Is there anyone there?" the man asked in an unsure voice. The man didn't know whether to question his eyes or his mind.

As the man was about to sit back down, a voice replied from the dark, "Peace, Simon, called Peter by Jesus the Risen Lord."

Peter, for that was the man's name, stepped back in surprise more than fear. A faint glow of white light grew in the corner, and it seemed to emanate from a man standing there robed in a tunic of shimmering silver.

"I bring a message from the one you have faithfully served: 'The end of your labor is near. Soon you will join the Savior and receive the crowns which have been laid up for you, but one task the Lord yet requires.'"

"Anything lord. Tell me what my Master requires, and it will be done with His strength to aid me."

The heavenly being stepped nearer and held out his hands, palms open to Peter. "These are the words of the Lord: 'A Light of hope and rest was given the world through My Son. My Church is established through Him and His followers. He performed works of wonder and healing during His time on earth. Since His ascension, similar works of wonder have been performed by those who proclaim them faithfully in His name. There will come a time when the people of the world will need restoration and reprieve. They will need guidance to the path of hope and salvation. But this age will lack great faith. Signs and wonders will seem a thing of the past. This age will require a voice to pray for wonders thought beyond the power of asking. Lend this age your voice, faithful servant, for I will heed your intersession.' Thus sayeth the Lord."

Peter stared at the angel, for that is what he knew him to be, not knowing what to say. He stroked his scraggly beard and finally said, "I understand I am to pray for an age that is not yet come, but I do not understand what I am to pray for or how I am to do it now."

"You will write a prayer of intersession for a world in need. The prayer will be read when the time of need is come."

"But I have no scroll or pen, and I still do not know what need I must pray for," Peter said somewhat exasperated.

"Ask the guard for what you require to write your prayer. Ask the Lord for guidance in wording your prayer. When you have finished, give your work to the guard and instruct him to take it to Himarius the merchant for keeping."

Without hesitation, Peter walked to the cell door and called to the guard. He was relieved to see that is was Caminus. Caminus was not a believer, but he had always been kind, if not respectful, to Peter.

"What is your need, Peter?" he asked as he walked to the cell door.

"I would ask a favor of you, Caminus."

"Name it, and it will be done if it is within my power and does not interfere with my duty."

Peter smiled. In many ways this young man was far more courteous than many believers he knew. "I would like to write something and was wondering if you might provide a scroll and pen."

"There is what you require in the shift room, but it will be poor in quality, for it is only used to send messages within the keep."

"That will be fine. Bring it at your convenience."

With that, Caminus walked back down the corridor. Peter turned back to his cell and found he was alone. He spent the next hour in prayer seeking the Lord's guidance in his task. A knock came at Peter's cell door that startled him from his supplication. Caminus was there with a small scroll, pen and ink, and a lighted candle.

"Thank you Caminus. You are a good man. I will remember you in my prayers."

Caminus said nothing but handed Peter the items, locked the cell door, and left. Peter began to write as soon as he was situated on the floor. The words flowed effortlessly onto the page in Peter's bold script. When he had finished, he rolled up the scroll and sealed it with wax from the candle.

That night when Caminus brought Peter's meal, Peter said, "I would ask one more favor of you."

"What is that?"

"It would be a great service to me if you would take this scroll to the merchant Himarius. Do you know him?"

"I know of him. He is a wealthy man, and it is said that his wealth is what protects his beliefs in Jesus of Nazareth. I will take it to him, but I would ask a favor in return."

"Yes?"

Caminus looked on Peter with eyes filled with serious curiosity. "I would have you explain to me your beliefs in God and if it is true that Jesus of Nazareth was His son."

Peter smiled at this request. He spent the rest of the night explaining the plan of salvation God had set before the world. In the morning, Caminus took the scroll to Himarius. He also carried a new faith in God and Jesus.

While Caminus was gone, guards came for Peter. He was led from Tullian Keep amid a throng of agitated people. The crowd stopped at a barren area outside the city. There, Peter was crucified upside down at his request, for he said that he did not deserve to hang as his Lord and Savior had on the cross. Thus ended the earthly life of Peter, the Apostle of Christ.

Chapter 1

Clip had a mile long list of things that got on his nerves, but a trip to the dentist ranked close to the top. It wasn't so much the fear of instruments or pain as much as the one sided conversations the dentist and hygienist who cleaned his teeth always had with him. It's hard to talk with a hand in your mouth, and Clip didn't think it was very sporting of them to ramble on asking questions and making comments when all he could do was grunt.

Clip didn't like being criticized either, and it seemed to him the hygienist must have taken a course in criticism at whatever training school she attended. According to her, he never flossed enough; he brushed the wrong way; or brushed too hard and damaged his gums. All the while she delivered these reprimands with her hand stuck in his mouth grasping a sharp instrument that could inflict a mortal wound when in the right hands.

The whole experience was getting on Clip's nerves more than usual today because he was going to be late meeting Mr. Estes—due mostly to the fact the hygienist was doing a lot more talking today than cleaning. Clip seized a moment when she reached for another instrument to speak, "Ms. Clangston, are you almost through? I've got to be somewhere by five."

"I'd be through by now Clip Tarence, if I didn't have to repair all the damage you do to your mouth in six months. So just sit back and pay the price for your lack of commitment to proper dental hygiene," she answered in a commanding tone.

"Yes Ma'am," Clip said more out of habit than respect. His nerve meter was at critical. One: at eighteen years of age, he didn't like being talked to like he was four. Two: his teeth were in fine shape. Actually, they were better than average. He figured arguing would only prolong the process, so he sat back and let her finish at what seemed now an even more sluggish pace.

After leaving the dentist's office, Clip jogged down the sidewalk that ran along the main street of Kawana, and hopped into his truck parked in the First Bank parking lot. Kawana was a small town in the Smoky Mountains of Tennessee. One road ran in and out of the town, and most people from Kawana hadn't been more than a day's drive down it in either direction. The people were good people though, big on heart but small on dreams. Kawana did have some perks you didn't find in most rural communities. Kawana was the Cherokee name for the area's largest mountain, so the name sort of grew with the town. This consequently led to the state funded natural history museum, with a Native American theme. Because of Kawana's central location, a small airstrip serviced wealthy sightseers flying in from Chattanooga, Knoxville, and Atlanta on small planes. One of the state's few operational drive-in movies could also be found on the south side of town.

Clip was going north this Friday evening in May. He was heading toward the foothills of the misty mountains where most of the residents of Kawana made their homes in the hollows and ridges of the Smokies. About a mile out of town, he passed the gravel road that led to his and his parent's home.

He loved his community and the mountains that towered around it. He always knew he would eventually settle down there and live his life like four generations of Tarences had done before him, but Clip also had a desire to see the world first, or at least part of it. Clip figure the first step toward this goal would be leaving for college.

He was fortunate enough to have the grades and financial backing to attend, within reason, any school in the country. Clip had graduated second in his class, and even though he was second out of just fifty-four, he was still proud of the accomplishment. Clip's parents were not rich, but they made a good living by Kawana standards. Clip's dad was principal of the high school, and his mom was head of nursing at the hospital. They had made sure Clip was well-read growing up, and they had traveled around the bordering states quite a bit. They had even taken an RV to California once.

But in Clip's mind, these trips were just glimpses of the world that was out there. He hungered for more than a glimpse. He wanted to be immersed in the land outside of Kawana, and he wanted to do it on his own, to see what he was made of when measured apart from Kawana standards.

Picking a college had been the first hurdle in this pursuit. In Clip's mind, college would be a springboard to the waiting world, and he put a monumental amount of time into researching for the perfect place to be educated, academically and otherwise.

Clip had also put a lot of prayer into his decision. He was a Christian, and to Clip that meant including God on the decision-making. Clip was not a predestined type of thinker. He didn't believe that God mapped a plan for your whole life, and you couldn't divert from it, even if you wanted. He did believe there was a loosely knit plan for one's life, but he also believed God would open doors of opportunity along the way if you only asked. To Clip it seemed a lot of people around him spent too much time sitting around waiting for "God's will" to drop into their lap, instead of just getting out there and going to work. In Clip's mind, God's will was to serve Him, and if you did your best to do that along life's way, there was no need to continually pray for a sign before taking any kind of action in your life.

Clip knew there were times to seek God's direction, but he also believed God gave you a brain in which to think and make decisions. This decision concerning college had been the biggest thus far in Clip's life, and he sought out every manner of help and aid, including asking God for wisdom and to open a door of opportunity.

In the end, Clip settled on Conn University. It was a private Christian college in a midsize city in Virginia. He had first heard about it from a missionary that spoke at his church. It was in the bulletin that he was an alumnus of Conn University, and on a whim, Clip had looked it up on the internet. He liked that it was a liberal arts school, and Conn had a good study abroad program. The fact that it was smaller in size also appealed to Clip. For all his need to explore the world beyond Kawana, he still had an affinity for the small town environment. Conn had accepted his application without a hitch, and he was even going to be on partial scholarship. His parents would pick up the rest.

Clip had felt relief ever since he had made the decision and often marveled at the way God always seemed to open these doors of opportunity for him. One such door had come his way in the spring a few years ago. It was the day he went to work for Mr. Estes.

Clip had first seen Mr. Estes at his church. An elderly man had come in just before the service started and occupied the end position on the back pew. The next few weeks he occupied that same spot on Sunday mornings, and though he arrived just before the service, he always stayed after and talked with many of the adults in the foyer. He seemed to be a jovial and outgoing man, but Clip never paid much attention to him.

After church one Sunday, Clip's dad asked him if he would like to earn some extra money.

"Sure. What do I have to do?"

"Have you seen the elderly man who has been visiting our church and sitting in the back?" he asked as they stepped out of their van and headed into the house.

"Yes, Sir. Kevin said his name was Mr. Estel, and that he was probably a drifter looking for help like that guy who showed up last summer."

Clip's dad grinned. "Estes, son. And I guess you could say he's a drifter of sorts but not like you think. He bought Charles Smith's old cabin as a vacation home. I've spoken to him the past couple of Sundays, and today he asked me if I knew somebody he could hire to watch after the place and take care of the yard and what not. I told him since we lived close-by, that my son might be interested."

"Hey! That'd be great, but does he know I'm just fourteen?" Clip asked with doubt in his eyes.

"I told him, and he didn't seem to mind. I also told him you would be by today to tell him one way or the other."

"Thanks dad!" Clip yelled already halfway to his room to change clothes.

The cabin Mr. Estes had bought was less than a mile's walk through the woods from Clip's house. Clip took long hurried strides as he tromped down the trail he had played on since he was a little kid.

The Smith cabin was built at the end of a dirt road in a little hollow. It was surrounded on the north and east by the foothills of the Kimsey Mountain range. The road into the hollow ran from the south, and on the west was a barrier of knolls and hills covered by hardwood trees. There was also a small, but active creek that ran down from the Kimseys and followed the road out of the hollow.

Clip came out of the dense hardwood forest on the west side of the cabin and found Mr. Estes rocking on the porch. He had a five-inch piece of pinewood in his left hand and a knife in his right. There was also a pile of shavings covering his lap and feet.

He looked up when he saw Clip draw near the rail. "You know, I haven't whittled in over fifty years. And I'm no better now than I was then. All I've managed to do is turn a perfectly good pine limb into an oversized toothpick." He stood up, and a shower of shavings fell to the porch floor. He leaned over the rail and stuck out his hand. "My name is Ralph Estes. You can call me Ralph."

"I reckon my dad would skin me if I did that Mr. Estes. My name is Clip Tarence, and you can call me Clip."

Mr. Estes smiled. He had a smile that looked natural, and well used. It looked even more natural than when he wasn't smiling. It was almost like he had to strain not to smile most of the time. "Well, nice to meet you *Mr. Tarence*. Your dad said you might be able to help me out with this place."

"Yes, sir. I can mow grass, trim shrubs, and use about any kind of tool there is."

"That will be fine indeed, Mr. Tarence. I basically just need the place kept up while I'm away and someone to keep an eye on everything for me. I won't be here much. Definitely not as much as I'd like to be. These mountains hold a lot of beauty and tranquility about them, but though I will be seventy-six this year, the Lord hasn't seen fit to sign my retirement papers yet."

Mr. Estes said this with a smile that belayed no discontent with his situation. "What do you do Mr. Estes?" Clip asked with mounting curiosity.

"I own a company that makes boats," he replied matter-of-factly. "Ski boats to be exact. I sell them all over the world and have to travel a lot. That's why I won't be here much."

"Don't you have salesmen that travel around and sell them for you?" Clip didn't know why, but Mr. Estes peaked his curiosity.

"Oh, yes. Hundreds I suppose. But I still like getting out and meeting people. You see Mr. Tarence, I'm a missionary of sorts. The Lord has blessed my business to the extent that many avenues are open for me to witness. You wouldn't believe how many government officials of big and small countries, CEO's, and other influential people are interested in water skiing. I meet many powerful men and women who think I have recreation to offer them. When in fact, I offer them the plan of salvation. It's hard for them to shrug you off when you're stuck in a boat in the middle of a lake."

Mr. Estes smiled that comfortable smile and invited Clip in for a glass of tea. They sat around his kitchen table drinking their tea and munching on graham crackers, and they talked more about themselves. Clip told Mr. Estes about his school, friends, and family. And Mr. Estes in turn told him about many of the places he had visited around the world and the people he met along the way.

Clip glanced at his watch a good while later and found he and Mr. Estes had talked most of the day away. "Well, I'd better be gettin' home Mr. Estes. We eat supper before Mom has to go to choir practice."

Mr. Estes thanked Clip for coming by and gave him a list of things he would like done around the property when Clip got the chance. He also gave him a key to the cabin and an admonition to do whatever he thought needed doing inside or outside the cabin. He told Clip that if he was agreeable to it, he would pay him a dollar above minimum wage. Clip just needed to keep up with his hours, and he and Clip could settle the bill when he came in every few weeks.

Clip was more than agreeable, and he thanked Mr. Estes for the job. They said their goodbyes, and Clip left for home feeling the achievement of landing a job and making a new friend. As he walked the trail, he pondered the weight of responsibility he felt. It was a good feeling. Clip also pondered Mr. Estes. There was something about his demeanor. There was something in his smile and eyes. Clip couldn't explain it then, but in the coming years he defined it as an understanding of life and purpose. It was a demeanor that Clip would strive for all his life.

Chapter 2

Ten minutes after he left the dentist's office, Clip turned onto the dirt road that led to Mr. Estes' cabin. When Clip had turned sixteen, he had started driving over to Mr. Estes' cabin to work or visit, and he had been down this road more times than he could count. Since the day he had been hired, Clip had been to the cabin three or four times a week to work or just check on the place. His cousin Holly, who was a year older, helped him clean the inside of the cabin every other week, and he billed Mr. Estes separately for this.

Sometimes Mr. Estes would not return for a couple of months to rest and recuperate from a trip, but when he did, he acted like the world would not turn without Clip's management of the place. This always made Clip feel important and responsible.

Clip pulled his truck in behind Mr. Estes' old, worn out van and bounded up the porch steps. There sat Mr. Estes, much as he had years earlier, whittling a piece of pinewood.

"Right on time Mr. Tarence," he said with his smile.

"That's me—Mr. Punctual. How was your trip?"

"Long. Hot. But then the monotony was broken by an increase in the humidity. All in all, not bad for Louisiana. I hear you've picked a university," Mr. Estes said with a knowing grin.

"Yes, sir. How'd you find out?"

"I stopped and talked with your parents on my way in."

Clip started to sit in one of the rocking chairs, but Mr. Estes stood and said, "Let's go inside, Clip. I've got something to show you."

This did not surprise Clip. Mr. Estes always brought

him something from his trips. He figured he was getting another souvenir, but Mr. Estes' demeanor seemed strange to Clip. He seemed stiff and very business like. He led Clip to the back bedroom, which had been converted to an office. There was a large mahogany desk against the far wall. In the two near corners, there were two overstuffed leather chairs. Mr. Estes scooted one, then the other to the desk. The desk had been cleared off, which seemed unusual to Clip.

Mr. Estes motioned for Clip to sit down in one of the chairs, and he followed suit. Mr. Estes' demeanor had changed now from businesslike to one of childish glee. He looked like a boy on Christmas morning ready to open presents.

"You know I have no children or family, Clip—at least no close family. Our friendship has come to mean a lot to me over the past few years, and while I am still able, I want to share something with you that is very precious to me."

A flood of emotion hit Clip. Excitement, uneasiness, and a sense of worry all swirled in Clip. "What do you mean, 'while you are still able?'"

"I'm getting old and weary, Clip. But I've lived a full life beyond my deserving. I can feel it in my bones that my years left are few."

"But you're not that old. Are you sick?" Clip asked starting to feel his emotions tipping toward shock and heartache.

"No. No." Mr. Estes said with a grin. "Unless you call old-age a sickness. I'm maybe not quite as young as you think I am. I'll be eighty-one my next birthday."

Clip knew Mr. Estes' age, but he had always seemed so vibrant to Clip that he never really considered him old.

"I want to tell you about something, Clip. And you may find it hard to believe at first. But what I am about to tell you changed my life . . . maybe *changed* is the wrong word. I guess I should say influenced me in a way that changed my outlook on life."

Clip was lost. He didn't understand where Mr. Estes was

going with this or what to expect next. The roller-coaster of emotions he was riding was already making him feel queasy.

Mr. Estes saw the confusion on Clip's face and said apologetically, "I'm sorry. You need an explanation of course, and for the explanation I must tell a story. The story is part of the life I've lived. It my take me a while to set the scene for you, Clip, but it is important in helping you understand; so please bear with me as I try and tell it as best as I can."

Clip's expression softened a little, and he sat back in his chair.

"About twenty years ago, Clip, I spent a great deal of time in England. My business was successful and self-sustaining. I had turned the reins of operation over to my nephew and decided I would give retirement a try. I had accomplished all the material goals I had set for myself and didn't know what to do next. As you know, I had no children or grandchildren to spend time with, so I looked for an outlet, and I found it in study.

"I had a hunger for knowledge, Clip. I always had a hunger for success, but once I had it, I needed something else to strive for. I contemplated what to do to fill the void. I realized that for all the traveling and meeting people I had done, I really didn't 'know' anything. I didn't know the history of the countries I visited, and I knew less about cultural intricacies. I had viewed the world in a business sense for sixty-one years, but I was blind to the humanity that made up the world. I don't know how else to explain it other than to say I felt like a dry sponge, and I yearned to soak up knowledge. Did you know I never went to college, Clip?"

Clip looked more than a little surprised. Mr. Estes always seemed so wise and successful. Clip just assumed he had a degree in business or something. "I never really thought about it," Clip replied. "I just figure you had."

"Well I didn't, and I was finding my success hollow. I wanted to put understanding and meaning to all I had accomplished. And at the risk of being a little melodramatic, I guess I wanted to put meaning to my existence, also. Now don't get me wrong—I was a Christian at this time, though a *weak* one. At that time in my life, I saw Christianity as a religion and didn't fully realize that Christianity is a relationship with God. If I had been wiser then, maybe I would have looked toward a greater knowledge of service to God instead of worldly knowledge. But it all worked out in the end.

"At any rate, I began a sort of quest. As corny as that sounds, that's how I saw it. I took on a quest to educate myself. I went to Oxford where I had a contact or two from my business dealings and began auditing courses. I took history classes, sociology classes, literature, economics, Greek, Latin, and even classes on religion. I visited museums across Europe and read incessantly. Still I hungered, Clip. I wanted 'it' so badly. The problem was, I couldn't define 'it.'

"During my travels of learning, I visited a monastery in the North Yorkshire region of England that had been built in 1802. It was called Stansberry Abby, and it had a college attached to it. I learned that the college was a small but prestigious private school, with about 500 students in attendance. The faculty was made up of talented professors as well as monks from the abbey. I was instantly drawn to the intimacy and relative seclusion of the setting. After a *small* donation to the college, I was allowed to attend classes. I was provided a room attached to the abbey itself in which to live, and for the most part, I was left to myself, except for a thirty-year-old monk by the name of Lohn. He taught a history class in the college, and we enjoyed discussing various things. I sought his insight of history, and he was fascinated in hearing a first hand account of countries he had only read about.

"One day he asked if I would like to accompany him to visit an old monk who lived alone in a remote part of the Northern Yorkshire Moors. I jumped at the chance to see some of the countryside. We took a bus to Oswaldkirk, and then hitched a ride a few miles outside of the village. Lohn had the driver stop by a dirt path that looked old but little used. We thanked the driver and started walking down the path that to me appeared to lead to nowhere.

"About three miles down the path, we came to a small, ancient looking building made of stone, with a thatched roof. There were windows on three sides with stone grates in them. Once we drew closer, I saw that the grates were actually carved crosses. There were wooden shutters on the inside, blocking the wind. The front of the building had a large oaken door with metal bands that held it together. Wisps of smoke rose from the stone chimney protruding from the roof. I felt as if I was in a sort of time-warp.

"Lohn told me that the building was called Han Milean and was once a type of monastery outpost where a single monk usually resided. It had been abandoned since the Dissolution of the monasteries by Henry the VIII in 1530, but the Brother we were visiting had repaired the stone remains and dwelt there for many years in solitude.

"Lohn knocked on the door, but there was no answer. He didn't seem surprised and we went on inside. The door opened to a sparsely adorned chamber that included the greater part of the building. There was a hearth with a low burning fire, an ancient looking table with a half loaf of partially molded bread and a slice of cheese on it. Another table had a water basin and cooking implements in neat order, and at the back of the room, was an entranceway to what looked like a small bedchamber. I also noticed at the far left corner of the chamber was another oaken door like the one we had just entered but much smaller. There was a large cast iron lock on the door. I marked it as unusual at the time but quickly forgot about it.

"Lohn seemed comfortable in the surroundings and soon busied himself with stoking the fire and preparing supper. I sat down in an old, worn chair beside the fire and started drowsing in the monotonous pulsing of the freshly stoked embers. I jumped awake from my half sleep when the huge door creaked open. In shuffled a little man wearing a well-worn robe made of gray and carrying a rabbit. A hooded tunic made of soft leather draped his head and shoulders. The little man removed the tunic and revealed a gaunt and aged face. Looking at him made me feel young again. Aged though it was, every wrinkle seemed to radiate from his smile. He ran a gnarled hand through his wispy head of white hair, gave it a few rubs back and said in a thick Scottish brogue, 'I guess you'll be wanting to share me rabbit then. Lucky for you lads I'm the able bodied hunter I am and snared two conies this evening.' With that he produced another rabbit from a sack hanging at his side.

"Lohn never turned from his task of preparing the meal but simply said, 'If you call walking to the other side of the hill and plucking a helpless animal from the many rabbit pens you have there an extraordinary feat of hunting, then you are dafter than the last time I was here old man.'

"The old gentleman laughed a full laugh and slapped Lohn on the back in a friendly fashion. 'I hope your friend has more manners than *you*, Brother Lohn.'

"Lohn said, 'That he does, and he also shares your obsession with study. Allow me to introduce Ralph Estes from America.'

"The old man bowed in the fashion of the older days. 'It is good to meet you *Rawlf*. How good, the night will tell. I am Brother Aaron.'

"I inclined my head and made an awkward bow in return. At this he laughed and ushered me outside to help him dress the rabbits. Aaron's outward appearance gave him to be a man of very many years, but joviality and dexterous movements belayed no sign of age. We had a hearty meal that night. I had never eaten rabbit before or many of the homegrown herbs used with the meal, but the tangy meat melted in my mouth as we sat at the table talking and eating leisurely.

"I slept that night on a pallet before the fire. The next day we roved the hills with Aaron picking an herb here and there and enjoying the clear day. We had another supper of good food and fellowship that night. I had quickly become comfortable with Aaron's jovial manner and zest for life. We took our leave of Aaron the next morning. Before we left, Aaron gave Lohn two or three old sheaves of parchment and some lined notebook paper filled with writing. I made no comment about this until we were walking down the road and my curiosity got the upper hand. Lohn answered my question quick enough. 'Aaron does a bit of translating for the monastery when the need arises. He's familiar with many languages and gets great satisfaction from studying and translating old documents.'

"I asked Lohn if that is what Aaron had given him. 'Yes. It was a bit of writing one of our brothers from a neighboring abbey came across. Aaron would translate a Greek grocery list if you found one.'

"I then asked the question that had been burning in me for two days. I wanted to know why he was out there in the middle of nowhere. It seemed to me that he would be in a scriptorium or library in one of the monasteries. 'For all his amiability, Aaron prefers the company of God alone,' Lohn said. 'He came here many years ago with the permission of the abbot. He's working on a project of sorts, though what it is I don't know. He sometimes travels to the monastery to borrow a book or two from the library and replenish his stationary supplies. Besides translating an odd document now and then, he keeps to his study in earnest.'

"I asked what the project was, but Lohn only shook his head and said, 'I don't rightly know. I've asked him a few times, and he just chuckles and says that it's an old man's pipe dream, nothing more.'

"That was all it took. I was hooked. I wanted to find out more than anything what Aaron found so compelling to isolate himself from the world to work on it. The next week I asked Lohn when he thought we might return to visit Aaron. He said probably in a couple of weeks. I must say I grew a little more impatient than common sense thought the situation warranted, but my gut curiosity kept fueling the fire. This was only the beginning of curious things to come."

Chapter 3

Mr. Estes returned from the kitchen with two glasses of iced tea and began again the telling of his story:

"True to word, Lohn and I left for Aaron's two weeks later. Lohn had some paper and pencils for Aaron, as well as a history text Aaron asked him to bring on his next visit. Aaron was there when we arrived. He was in the back room that had been locked on my first visit. He came out of the room when he heard us enter, and though he did not lock it back, I did notice he closed the door behind him.

"Aaron seemed pleased with our visit, although after what Lohn told me, I wasn't sure if it was us or the things we brought *for* him he was happy to see. We spent the next two days much as we had on our last visit. The morning we were to depart, I surprised Lohn by expressing my desire to stay another day or two to do some thinking in the peace Han Milean. Aaron looked at me curiously and said, 'I have no objection, though I'm afraid I am not much of a host. I work in my study most of the day.'

"I told him I required no special attention, and that I only wanted to steal some of the quiet repose. He smiled at this and said, 'There's plenty of that lad. Though we may find what kind of cook ye be.'

"So began my friendship with Aaron. It was cordial at first. I spent a week at Han Milean, and as he predicted, I only saw Aaron at meals. The rest of the time he stayed holed up in his study. I wandered the hills, read a couple of books I brought, and I prayed. I found myself seeking a closer relationship with God that week. I started understanding what Aaron had meant by preferring the company of God. It was nice to sit, think, and express my prayers in a more conversational manner than my normal ritualistic dialogue.

"I went back to the monastery, but I returned to Han Milean two weeks later. I felt drawn to the solitude, and my curiosity had not abated either. My first night back I asked Aaron about his work during our supper. Without looking up from his plate, he said between mouthfuls, 'Mmm . . . an old man's dream, nothing more. I'm afraid you would find it tedious and a bit boring.'

"I told him to try me, but he did not reply, so I assumed he had dropped the subject. The next morning Aaron was in his study before breakfast. I had just laid some scrambled eggs and slices of cheese on the table when Aaron strode into the room carrying a book, some paper, pencils, and a very old looking sheaf of parchment. 'Rawlf, can you read Latin?' The question caught me so off guard that I just looked at him for a moment. Aaron sat down and started eating the eggs as if he hadn't said anything.

"I stammered around a minute about auditing some courses at Oxford but not with much proficiency. I asked him why he wanted to know, and he said, 'I remembered you saying something about taking a course or two, and I thought you might do a wee bit of translating today. Here's a book to help you.' With that, he took the rest of his meal into his study without another word. I sat there half excited, half bewildered. I cleared off the table and went to work.

"The book Aaron had laid on the table was an ancient English/Latin dictionary with some verb tenses in the back. After many hours of labor, I produced a one-page translation of what appeared to be a will. The document mentioned a few possessions and birthrights. It wasn't exciting reading, but the idea of studying an apparently old document from a far off land excited me.

"That evening when Aaron came out for supper, he examined my work. 'Not too bad for a beginner. I guess you found it pretty dull though?'

"I told him that I found it very interesting, and I asked him if he thought I could try some more. He said he might find a scrap or two that I might find more interesting, and for the next month, I spent my days translating manuscripts that were either pieces of other lost documents or mundane events and transactions. Aaron and I also spent a great deal of time roaming the moors and talking about various subjects ranging from philosophy to theology. Aaron had been spending much less time in his study, and this afforded us more time to establish a closer friendship.

"Lohn paid a visit about this time and brought with him an old looking sheet of parchment that had been partially burned. The writing on it was written in a bold script. Lohn said it was found during the remodeling of a cellar at a home near Stansberry Abbey. The man who found it had a firm belief it would reveal something of important historical significance.

"Aaron looked at the document with mild interest and was about to share with me what it said, for Lohn was quite fluent in Latin; as were all the monks at the abbey, when I asked if I could translate it. Lohn looked surprised at this request and said, 'So you've got Ralph on the payroll now, eh?'

"I told him Aaron had been letting me translate some things, though I was very slow at it. Aaron handed the manuscript to me and said, 'Speed is no substitute for quality, lad. You can give this one a try if you'd like. That is if you've got a week to wait on it, Lohn?' They both chuckled, and I began at once working on the translation. By supper I had the short document ready for Aaron's inspection. He held the two works side by side and compared them. After a few moments, he handed my translation to Lohn for him to read.

"'Do you recognize the words?' Aaron directed the question to me. The words were beautiful and poetic, and though the tone was familiar to me, I did not recognize the sentences themselves. Lohn seemed to read the words knowingly, but I replied that I did not and asked if I should.

"Lohn handed the translation back to Aaron and said, 'It is part of the 104th Psalm.'

"Aaron nodded his head. 'The first nine verses to be exact.' He elaborated for my benefit.

"I felt slightly embarrassed and ashamed at my apparent lack of Biblical knowledge in the presence of these devoted and astute men of God. Nothing more was said of the translation that night, and the next day as Lohn was preparing to leave, he asked me if I would be joining him. 'Actually, I was hoping Rawlf might stay and help me with a bit of work,' Aaron said as he folded a letter to the abbot at Han Milean.

"Lohn took his leave, and Aaron, and I spent the rest of the day repairing the rabbit pens and weeding the garden. I decided this was the work he had mentioned to Lohn. In the morning, we ate breakfast, and afterwards Aaron went into his study and left me to clear the table. In a few moments he returned with the old Latin dictionary and a wooden box. His demeanor seemed changed from only a few moments ago. He seemed stern. He also looked apprehensive, as if there was an internal debate going on inside him. At one point, he stopped halfway across the room, shook his head, and then continued to the table. He put the book down and then gingerly set the box beside it. He took a white cloth from his pocket and spread it on the table. He opened the box. The lid had a wax seal around the edges. I assumed this was to keep it airtight. He slowly removed a scroll and laid it on the cloth. Then he went to a shelf and retrieved some paper and a pencil, pulled a chair back from the table, and said to me: 'Will you translate this?'

"It was more than a question of whether I would perform a task. The earnestness of his voice belayed a sense of responsibility that came with the task. It was a responsibility that I could not understand at the time. I didn't say a word. I simply sat down and clasped the edges of the table with my hands. My actions were answer enough, and I felt the weight of the moment pressing against me on all sides. Aaron walked to a chair by the fire and sat down staring at the embers of the morning cook fire. I began my work with timid concentration. It was a bit disconcerting having Aaron there in the room while I worked. I felt like a small child again taking a test in school. When I finished translating the first line, I dropped my pencil and sat erect in my chair. I looked at Aaron, and he turned toward me with a half smile on his lips and in his eyes. I looked back down at what I had just written and read it again: *I, Stephen, servant of God, leave here guidance to the location of the three scrolls that contain the prayers of the Apostles. Inspired by the Lord Himself, may He render their finding by true servants in His time.*

"I asked Aaron if the scroll was real and what it meant. He paused before speaking. It appeared as if one last internal debate was still in question, but it seemed once Aaron became resolved in his decision a fire was kindled in him. He jumped from his chair and leaned over the table and looked me square in the eye and said, 'It is indeed real.'

"I asked again what it meant and where he got it. He held up his hand to stop my flow of questions and said, 'Patience, lad. Patience.' He moved to a chair at the table and sat down. He reached toward the old scroll and ever so gently caressed the edges. 'I'll start with your first question. Yes, it is real. And for your second question: two days before he died, an old monk named Janarius gave me a box that contained this scroll and another. He was a great mentor and friend to me. I will confess that I was even more shocked and skeptical than you are now, but I will tell you the story as it was told to me. Janarius was very secretive about the whole business. I was warned against sharing knowledge of the prayer scrolls. The scrolls came forth from the treasuries of the Byzantine Empire just before its fall in the 15th century. The Church was unsure of the power of the prayers and had originally sought to suppress the knowledge of their existence. Soon, they became pawns of power within the church, and factions saw them as tools of self edification.'

"I asked what power could lie in the prayers that would be so valuable.

"'On the scrolls are written prayers of supplication by three Apostles for a world in need. God Himself inspired the prayers. They are an intercession for the world when faith is weak and signs and wonders are thought a thing of the past. It is believed that when the scrolls are read aloud that God will answer the prayer of his faithful servants written almost 2000 years ago.'

"I asked him where the scrolls were. He answered, 'The location of the scrolls is a secret I confess I do not know, but the key lies in the second scroll that was given to me by Janarius. The scroll contains the directions to the location of the prayers. You see around the early 1500's, there was a group of priests, five in all, who feared the misuse of the scrolls. The priests undertook to hide the scrolls so that the Church would not use them as tools of power to hold over the heads of the world. These priests saw the prayers as tools of hope. The priests took the scrolls and then the priests were dispersed across the nations with the expressed intention to hide them, and in some cases, they entrusted the keeping of the prayers to trusted believers who were to keep the scrolls safe until someone returned for them. The priests met again in Rome to record the locations of the hidden documents—the prayers. They noted each location, and the directions to the various hiding places were given to the youngest priest among them. This priest went into hiding, and soon, the four other priests were found out by the Church. They were then imprisoned until one of them would tell where the prayers were hidden. All four of the priests died in confinement.'

"Aaron paused before he began again. It appeared the story moved him deeply, and I assumed this was the first time he had spoken of it aloud. In a moment he began again. 'Eventually, the prayers became a memory and then forgotten completely by the Church. The directions passed down from one trusted believer to the next for over 500 years until they fell to me.'

"I asked Aaron why no one had used the directions to collect the prayers. He replied, 'There's the rub, lad. The directions are in a code. The young monk who went into hiding feared if something ever happened to him that the prayers would fall into the wrong hands, whether the Church or someone else.'

"Of course I was drawn further into the mystery, and I asked to see the code. Aaron led me to his study. It was a very surreal feeling entering that room. I couldn't count the times I'd have given anything for a peek in there. There were papers and books in organized stacks on a number of shelves and small tables. By the window, there was an old desk and chair with an oil lamp. On the desk was a box about two feet in length and one foot wide. I knew it to be the box Aaron had been given. There was a symbol etched in the lid. It looked like a fish with a small cross for an eye. Aaron strode quickly to the box. He sat down in the chair and gently opened the lid. I noticed the edges of the lid had a seal like the other box. He took out the old scroll and unrolled it on the cloth on the desk. There were Roman numerals all over the scroll. Some were grouped. Some were by themselves.

"Aaron's eyes scanned the scroll. 'This is it. Though what *it* is I haven't been able to figure out for many years.'

"I was surprised by this. I took it for granted that there was nothing that could stump Aaron. 'The good Lord knows I've tried to learn what it means,' he said with a sigh. 'I have studied, compared, and prayed over this scroll since it came to me. I wanted so badly to unlock the secret of the code, but it may not be my lot to discover it.'

"I asked him what he meant by this. He replied, 'Along with the passing of the diary and the directions also passed this knowledge: It is said that the young priest who went into hiding was so worried the prayers would be discovered that he prayed fervently to God to give him a means of encoding the directions until the time the prayers should be revealed again. God granted his request, and in a spurt of inspiration, the young priest began writing down these numbers. When he had finished, he himself did not know their meaning. But he trusted it was inspired by God and burned the only remaining copy of the directions. None of the Keepers have ever deciphered the code, though it has been an exercise for many long centuries.'

"I told him I had only one more question for the time being, but he beat me to the punch. 'Why you?' he said, finishing my thought. I asked him why he did not pick someone like Lohn, someone more holy than me.

"He smiled and answered, 'Don't think I divulge this secret lightly, my friend. There are many *holy* men out there, and others with talents and abilities beyond yours and mine. But I see something in you lad that is a rare quality. You have a willingness to be used. In our conversations, I sense you search for a meaningful role in life beyond wealth. There is no greater service than being an instrument of the Kingdom. I wish you to be the next Keeper.'

"I didn't know how to respond. This seemed to be the purpose that I had been searching.

"Aaron continued to work tirelessly on breaking the code, with no success. The days rolled by, and I saw a change in Aaron. He had little patience with even trivial things. He spent more and more time in his study. The enthusiasm that spilled forth from him after divulging the secret of the prayers was being replaced with a restlessness that ever increased. I asked if I could help, but he said he himself was on no path, so there was none to which he could steer me.

"I suggested he take a break one morning and join me for a walk through the hills. It was mid-autumn, and there was a bite in the wind that revived the sluggishness from being cooped up inside. We returned that evening and had a pleasant supper. We talked like we used to, about world events far away and debated points of Scripture. At one point, Aaron adamantly stood by a point of doctrine I was sure I could refute by showing him a passage of Scripture. I opened my Bible and turned to the passage.

Aaron looked at it, and I was waiting for him to concede my point when I noticed he was scanning the margins of the page. I asked him if he was too stubborn to admit I had a point. He didn't answer for a minute, and I was getting a little perturbed. Finally, he said, 'What are the Scripture numbers printed in the margin?'

"I told him that it was a study Bible, and they were references to other scriptures that might relate to that passage. He furrowed his brow and looked contemplative. He turned from me, stared at the far wall, and began talking to himself, 'Hmmm ... I wonder? No. That can't be right.'

"I asked him what he was talking about. I was getting confused by his words and actions. 'The scroll of directions,' he said. 'I've compared it to all the knowledge of the time it was written. I have never compared it to a modern day Bible because it was not printed in its current form until the King James Bible was printed in 1611, almost 100 years after the young priest wrote the code. Aye, it would have to be divinely inspired indeed if it related to the modern day Bible.'

"With that, he sprung from his chair with more enthusiasm than I had seen since the day he told me of the prayers. That was the day we began our long, difficult labor."

Chapter 4

Clip sat motionless in his chair. He had been listening to Mr. Estes for the better part of the evening, and now that he was through speaking, Clip didn't know what to say. He had always put a lot of trust in Mr. Estes and valued his opinion. But he had just told Clip a story that seemed a little out there. Mr. Estes looked expectantly at Clip.

"Do you have any questions?"

"Well, was it the answer to the code . . . the Bible I mean?" Clip asked.

"Yes. But it was not near as easy as we thought it might have been. The Roman numerals were references to specific books, chapters, and verses, but there was nothing to indicate which word or words were to be used. We had to try the words that seemed to fit. Sometimes it was obvious which word would be used, but many times we had to try each one and fit it together like a puzzle."

"But you did figure it out?"

"Yes. Eventually. It took fifteen years to complete the task. Sadly, Aaron never saw the finished product. He died five years after we began."

"So you finished it yourself?" Clip looked surprised.

Mr. Estes laughed. "Heavens no! I knew I couldn't do it by myself. I'm not much of a scholar; no matter how much money I donate to universities. I also knew I needed guidance on what to do with the prayers if I ever found them, so I told Lohn everything. I returned to Stansberry, and we spent the next ten years decoding the scroll, but that was only half the battle."

"What do you mean?"

"The directions do not give specific locations. They are

very general. They define more of an area than 'x marks the spot' as they say."

"Well, did you go after them?" Clip asked as his enthusiasm rose, and he now warmed to the mystery as Mr. Estes had so many years ago.

"It wasn't that simple at the time. A few years after Aaron's death, word came to me that I needed to contact my home office immediately. Apparently I had placed too much trust in my nephew. He had embezzled a large sum of money from the company and left for parts unknown. I couldn't stand to let something I had worked so hard to build, fall by the wayside. Nor could I let hundreds of employees lose their jobs, so I returned and tried to put the pieces back together. Lohn and I both continued to work on the locations of the scrolls. I visited him several times a year, and after five years of work, and many emails between us, we decided we had pinpointed the locations as close as we could."

"Why didn't you go look for one when you figured out a location?"

"We thought about it several times, but it didn't seem right to either of us. In the end, we felt what we were undertaking should be completed in stages, and figuring out the locations of all the prayers was only one of the stages."

"So what did you do next?"

"Well, let's see. By this time, I had my company back on its feet, and I moved here to Kawana. You never knew it, but a year after moving here, I sold my company to a Christian businessman I had known for years. Kawana was supposed to be a base of operations for the plan Lohn and I had decided on. We realized we were not 'spring chickens' anymore and determined to find one person each to entrust the secret to and help us carry on with the next stage. We both took this very seriously. We wanted to find two young Christians of character and commitment. I tell you now; I've traveled all across the U.S. in my search. I visited colleges, seminaries, military academies, and every other place where a steadfast youth might be found."

"So all those times I thought you were gone on business trips, you were just traveling around looking for somebody?"

"Yes, and what I didn't realize was what I sought was under my nose the whole time."

It finally registered with Clip what Mr. Estes was getting at. "*You* are the one, Clip. You are the one to whom I'm entrusting the secret."

Clip had never thought of himself as 'steadfast, committed or any of the other things Mr. Estes mentioned. Sure, he was a Christian, and he tried to live like he thought God wanted. But he didn't see himself as a worthy enough person to be entrusted with this knowledge.

While Clip had been contemplating these thoughts, Mr. Estes had risen from his chair and retrieved a silver briefcase from the closet. The briefcase had a matte finish and reminded Clip of ones you saw in spy movies that contained a bomb or top-secret documents. Mr. Estes sat the briefcase on the desk, then laid his old worn hand on the briefcase and patted it lovingly like one might pat the head of a child. His aged fingers fumbled with the combination until he had the numbers aligned correctly. With a quick *snap,* the latches released, and Mr. Estes opened it. There was gray foam padding on the inside. In the center of the case was a square box made of heavy plastic that was sealed around the edges by a molded lid. Mr. Estes lifted the box from the briefcase and placed it on the desk. He took out a white cloth that had been folded under the box and spread it on the table in front of Clip. He opened the box and removed a scroll and placed it on the cloth.

Mr. Estes turned to Clip. "Go ahead. Take a look."

Clip slid his chair closer to the table and scanned the scroll. It was written in Latin. Clip had taken two courses in high school at the urging of Mr. Estes, so he could pick out several of the words on the scroll. He knew it to be the scroll written by the priest named Stephen who had also written the code. Mr. Estes then removed from the briefcase another scroll covered with Roman numerals. He placed it on the table beside the other scroll, and Clip knew it to be the coded directions.

"Now what?" Clip asked.

"Now we take a trip. If you are willing?"

"Of course I'm willing! Where are we going, and when do we leave!" Clip had risen from his chair as if a plane was waiting in the yard to take off any minute.

Mr. Estes laughed. "Soon. Soon. You still have a week until graduation. We will leave the day after that. Of course we have to get your parents' approval."

"That will be no problem. But what will we tell them?"

"We can't tell them about the scrolls of course . . . at least not yet." Mr. Estes replied. "But I don't think they will object to you *touring* some countries with me this summer. I will tell them it will be my graduation present to you."

Clip didn't know what to say. His head was reeling with it all. "Are we going to get the scrolls?"

"Eventually. Hopefully. But we will first meet Lohn and the person *he* has chosen to keep the secret."

"Do you know him?" Clip asked.

"I have met him several times. He is a bright young man named Jamisen. He grew up near Stansberry and resides there now. He has known of the secret for several months now."

Clip left Mr. Estes' home well after dark. He had a never-ending supply of questions, but Mr. Estes told him to be patient and absorb what he had already learned. There would be time for more questions on the trip to Stansberry where they were meeting Lohn and Jamisen.

CHAPTER 5

Clip's parents had whole-heartedly approved of the opportunity, so the next week was spent in preparation for the trip. Mr. Estes took Clip on a shopping spree of sorts in the nearest big city, Chattanooga. He bought Clip three outfits of what he called "traveling clothes." Everything was thin, lightweight and easy to pack. The pants were of a type Clip had seen in sporting magazines where the bottom half of the pants could be zipped off to convert the pants to shorts. He also bought Clip a pair of expensive hiking shoes and a backpack in which to carry all his things.

Based on his extensive travel experience, Mr. Estes had admonished Clip to only pack what would fit in the backpack and would be of necessity. It had taken Clip several attempts to narrow his belongings down to a sufficient number to fit in the pack. In the end, he took: the clothes Mr. Estes had bought him, two extra pairs of underwear and socks, a digital camera his parents had bought him for the trip, a pocket knife, a small bag of toiletry items, sun glasses, a small Bible, a tan cap with a big orange "T" on it for the University of Tennessee, a small flashlight, and finally a leather bound journal and pen to write down his experiences. In the end, he actually had a little room to spare, which he figured allowed for any thing extra he might pick up along the way. Mr. Estes had a similar pack to Clip's and carried the silver briefcase that contained the scrolls. He gave Clip another leather briefcase to carry that contained a laptop, maps, and papers that related to Mr. Estes' years of study.

Mr. Estes left his van at the cabin, and Clip's parents drove them to the airport in Atlanta about two hours away. There was a tearful goodbye and just the slightest moment of hesitation in the back of Clip's mind. He felt like he was standing on the other side of a great line, and once he crossed it there would be no turning back. But the thought only lasted a moment, and the two companions were off.

The only hitch in the whole departure came at the security checkpoint. Clip's pocketknife set off the alarm, and security made him put it in a large, brown envelope and mail it back to Kawana. Clip was embarrassed beyond belief, but Mr. Estes only laughed. They boarded the plane and took their seats in first class. Mr. Estes confessed that usually he flew coach, but first class provided them with more privacy to talk.

This was one of the nuances about Mr. Estes that Clip never understood. Clip always figured a man of Mr. Estes' wealth would have the best of the best and would travel in luxury. But Mr. Estes owned nothing flashy as far as Clip could tell. He drove an old dodge van, with over 200,000 miles on it. He wore simple clothes with no designer labels. He never made mention of his money except in the most abstract sense. To Clip this seemed to go against all the stereotypes of rich people you see on TV and in the movies.

Clip had never flown before, and when the plane took off, the slight pressure he felt pushing him back into his seat was like a starting pistol going off in his head. "This is it! I'm on my way!" Clip had never felt such an adrenaline rush. He was young, carefree, and setting out on journey the consequences of which he still could not fully comprehend.

Clip and Mr. Estes talked the plane ride away in hushed tones. Mr. Estes was eager to fill in any of the blanks he had left out concerning the history of the scrolls and eager to answer all of Clip's questions, which were many. At one point in the conversation, Mr. Estes reached for his billfold and pulled out a business card. "I had almost forgotten to give you this. I want you to take this and keep it in a safe place with you at all times," Mr. Estes said as he handed Clip the card.

On it was written:
Mark Stone, Attorney at Law

Home: 256–837–4052
Work: 256–837–7004
Cell: 828–455–9434
Pager: 828–496–1936

"What's this?"

"This is in case of an emergency. Mark and I have been friends for many years. He knows everything about me with the exception of the scrolls. If you are ever in any trouble or need help and I am not around, call Mark at any time. He has access to my accounts and can send help wherever you are." Clip was staring at the card oddly. "You will probably never need to use it, but I will feel better knowing you have it just in case."

Their plane landed in London on a damp May evening, and they checked into what Clip thought was a pretty ordinary hotel. The night sounds were about all Clip was able to experience of London, for in the morning they boarded a domestic flight to Leeds/Bradford airport. From there they took a bus to a station in a small village a mile from Stansberry. They walked only a short distance toward the abbey before someone offered them a lift.

The abbey was not at all like Clip had pictured it in his mind. For some reason he envisioned small stone buildings with no electricity and little shaven head men in robes solemnly walking around. Only a fragment of this was accurate. The buildings were made of stone, but they were large two and three story structures with sweeping arches. Cobblestone pathways connected the buildings, and manicured lawns and shrubbery filled the spaces between where a path and building did not occupy. The land surrounding the abbey was an endless visage of rolling hills with clumps of hardwood trees here and there like little islands in an ocean of green.

There were two main clusters of buildings that were separated by a large courtyard. Mr. Estes pointed to the cluster on the right as they started up the main driveway that led to the abbey. This, he said, was the abbey itself, which housed the monks and their small business operations, including a print shop and a hospitality room for visitors. To the left was the college, which had recently been adapted to co-ed status. As they drew nearer to the buildings, Clip could see a marked difference in the college and the abbey that could not be discerned from far away. The college was of definite newer construction, while the abbey had a look of antiquity. There were men in robes to be seen walking here and there or sitting and talking, but they looked anything but solemn to Clip. To him they actually looked like normal people going about normal things, only they wore light grey robes made of a terry cloth looking material. There were also many more men and women alike to be found mingling around the courtyard and in and out of the buildings. To Clip it looked like many of the colleges he had visited in America.

Mr. Estes made straight for the abbey and was greeted by almost all the people they passed along the way. He took no time to explain to Clip any of the twists and turns he took. It seemed he had a renewed spring in his step and was eager to find Lohn. After navigating the maze work of halls and stairways, they arrived at the door to what appeared to be a small living cell of one of the monks. The door was partially opened and a large man in a robe could be seen hunched over a table writing. Mr. Estes knocked on the door and entered simultaneously. The large man turned around and jumped from the chair almost knocking it down.

"Ralph! You are here at last. Heaven be praised for your safe journey. And this must be Clip. Hello, my son."

"Hello." Clip put down the briefcase and extended his hand. Lohn took it and swallowed Clip's in his giant paw and shook it furiously.

"I can tell by the handshake, at least, you have chosen a good one, Ralph. Most of these young ones today feel like they are handing you a dead fish when they shake your hand, but this one has some vitality about him."

Lohn's smile could not be hid behind his bushy, brown

beard that contained streaks of gray. He looked to be in his mid-forties, with a large frame that was made up of more muscle than flab. He asked them to sit down. Clip had to sit on the bed as the room had only one other chair. "Well, Clip. I feel like I know you already from all that Ralph has told me through the past couple of years, but it is good to finally put a face to all his 'yammerings.'"

"I hope you don't believe all he told you," Clip said with a grin.

"Only the bad, my son," Lohn replied as he winked at Mr. Estes.

"Well, Lohn. Have you any news?" Mr. Estes asked. But before he could answer a knock came at the door and a young man wearing a grey robe similar to Lohn's entered at Lohn's acknowledgement.

"Ho, good timing. We can finish the introductions with one fell swoop. Clip, this is Jamisen. He is a Novice monk and co-conspirator in our undertaking."

Jamisen looked to be about Clip's age. He was tall, with an athletic build. His hair was brown and curly. He had an affable smile and threw up his hand in greeting, and he offered a genuine, "Hello." This stuck in Clip's mind, for so many people Clip had encountered in his life often said 'hello' out of habit or courtesy and nothing more. Jamisen said it in a way the made Clip feel like he was really pleased to see them.

"You asked for news, Ralph, but I'm afraid I might have some bad news."

"What is it?"

"I'm not sure it is anything at the moment. In fact, I am almost completely sure it is nothing, but it has nagged at the back of my mind for a few days now."

Mr. Estes straightened in his chair more out of curiosity than impatience. "Are you going to tell us, or are we to guess?"

"Patience is still not a virtue you have learned in all your study, Ralph," Lohn said grinning. "OK. Here it is. A few days ago Jamisen and I were sitting on a bench in the rose garden having what we thought was a private conversation concerning the scrolls. It was very early in the morning, just after sun up. We had not seen anyone around and thought we were alone. But as we left, I saw someone sitting on a bench that was obscured by a trellis that was directly behind us. The person had obviously been sitting there before we arrived. I don't think he heard anything or could have understood what we were talking about anyway."

"Who was it?" A look of anxiety was beginning to spread across Mr. Estes' face.

"Well, that might be the only catch. It was a visiting bishop from the Vatican. He is visiting several abbeys across England. His name is Bishop Sorlenni. I spoke to him as Jamisen and I left, and he made no comment about our conversation. We spoke a few pleasantries and that was it. I really don't feel there is anything to worry about."

Mr. Estes looked contemplative and then said in a more relaxed tone, "You are probably right. Even if he did hear you conversation I don't think he could discern anything from it. The scrolls have been out of memory for centuries now."

Lohn rose. His affable grin returned and said, "Come. You are probably hungry. We will get something to eat and let everyone get more acquainted."

They left the room feeling at ease about the minor slip-up, but they would soon find out the scrolls had not passed from *everyone's* memory.

Chapter 6

The next two days were spent in preparation for the first expedition to find the scrolls. Late on the second night the four met in Mr. Estes' room to study the directions to the first scroll they were going to try and find. Spread on the table were maps and a piece of paper with several short lines written on it. It was this paper that they were studying.

Mr. Estes read the lines out loud:
To the east lies a nation of many people.
Its borders are a wall and the sea.
Follow the road of silk to the second temple
of God built in the land.
It is a Nest at the footstep of a pagan belief.
Tread 300 in the way of the fish.

Clip listened to Mr. Estes and then looked at the lines and read them silently to himself. The mysterious lines meant nothing to him, other than it referred to some country in the east. But east of what, he did not know. "I hope you have already figured it out because I don't have the foggiest idea of where it is talking about. It seems very vague."

Lohn chuckled. If it was easy to figure out, it wouldn't have taken so many years to decipher it. Of course, Ralph and I are not what you would call brilliant scholars either."

Clip knew better, as did Jamisen who chimed in, "Well, will you explain it to us, or are we to discuss the failings of your scholarship all night."

"OK. OK," Mr. Estes laughed as he sat down at the table and underlined the first line. "These are the words that we found from the verses that made the most sense:
To the east lies a nation of many people. What country

do you know of that lies in the east that is known for having millions, even billions of people?"

"China," answered Jamisen quickly.

"Right," Mr. Estes continued. "*Its borders are a wall and the sea.*"

"The wall is the Great Wall of China built on the western side of the country, and the East China Sea borders the eastern side of the country," Jamisen said confidently.

"Right again, Jamisen. You know your geography."

Clip was beginning to feel like the dunce of the class. Jamisen seemed to be quite a bit more learned than he. Mr. Estes underlined the third line and read it aloud, "*Follow the road of silk to the second temple of God built in the land.*"

Mr. Estes looked at Jamisen expectantly. Jamisen just shrugged and said, "I never heard of any roads being made of silk."

Something clicked in Clip's mind and he offered, "Is it talking about the trading route that used to be called the *Silk Road?* I think it ran from somewhere in the Middle East to China."

"Excellent, Mr. Tarence! You are absolutely right as far as we can deduce."

Clip felt pleased to finally appear to have a little on the ball. "I don't know about *the second temple of God* part though," he said as he scrutinized the paper.

"That and the next line are where it gets a little tricky," answered Mr. Estes. "The second known Christian church or *temple* in China was thought to be discovered six years ago by a British expert on Chinese history and culture. This man also happened to be a theologian, so he took particular interest in any Christian influence that could be discovered in Chinese history. The site of the church resides fifty miles outside of the city of Xi'an. It is called the 'Daqin pagoda.' It is located among Taoist temples that were built during the same time period. Now comes the tricky part. The line: *It is a Nest at the footstep of a pagan belief* perplexed us greatly until we figured out the part concerning the second church.

"There was a stone discovered in Xi'an in the 1600's that tells of the early Christian movement that was established all across China. It is called the Nestorian Stone, named after a prominent priest of the time—the stone was carved in the eighth century. Ever sense the discovery of this stone, Christians in this part of the world and of that time the church was built were called Nestorians. So the *Nest at the footstep of a pagan belief* reaffirms that it is this ancient church located among the pagan Taoist temples."

"How did you figure this out?" asked Jamisen more than a little confused.

"Luck, really," said Mr. Estes. "I read an article in a magazine written about the British expert finding the site of the second oldest Christian church in China, and most scholars who study the history of Christianity know about the Nestorian Stone, including Lohn. The *Nest* part made sense after I showed the article to him. The *Nest* refers to the Nestorian Christians who built the church. Lao-Tzu was said to have founded Taoism in this same area of the temples. *At the footstep of a pagan belief* refers to the church built near the Taoist temples."

"All right. What about the *Tread 300 in the way of the fish*. What does that mean?" Clip asked.

Mr. Estes and Lohn looked at each other apprehensively until Lohn finally spoke. "That's a small snag we ran into. We hope that part will be evident when you reach the site of the church. Hopefully there will be some kind of clues to figure it out. For now, it is as close as we can come to pinpointing the location."

"OK, gentlemen. I suggest we adjourn and get a good night's sleep before setting out tomorrow."

"I agree, Ralph," said Lohn.

Clip and Jamisen headed to their rooms, and Mr. Estes followed after a few more minutes of discussion with Lohn.

"Do you think they are ready, Ralph? Do you think they even understand?"

"Can anyone truly comprehend what we might discover? I think they will be fine. I'm more worried about myself to be honest. All these years of preparation, and when it finally comes to it, I don't know if my old body is up for it."

"Ha, Ha. You are much too stubborn to allow that my friend, though I think we will all need God's strength before the end of this endeavor. Let us pray for it now on the eve of the journey."

After a humble plea to God for strength and guidance, Lohn also left for his room. When he reached his door, he noticed it was ajar. When he entered, he found Bishop Sorlenni sitting in a chair with his arms folded and his legs crossed.

He rose with a smile and said in a thick Italian accent: "Ah, Brother Lohn. I am sorry to have intruded, but I wanted to speak with you in private before you went to bed."

"Quite all right. I am just returning from praying," Lohn said truthfully. "What did you want to speak to me about?" Lohn's stomach was as tight as a vice.

"I was wondering if you know anything about the ancient Prayer Scrolls of the Apostles?"

Chapter 7

Clip and Jamisen met for breakfast the next morning. They were both excited about the start of the journey. They talked and laughed through the meal. Both young men were becoming more comfortable in the other's company. After the meal, they hurried to Lohn's room. They found Lohn and Mr. Estes in the midst of a serious conversation. Both of the older men were startled at their entrance.

"Oh. Hello, boys. Have a seat. We have a new development that Lohn and I were just discussing. It appears that Bishop Sorlenni heard and understood more than we thought."

"What happened?" asked Jamisen.

"Bishop Sorlenni was waiting in my room last night after we met. He asked me about the scrolls."

"What did you say?" blurted Clip.

"I told the truth." Clip and Jamisen both looked alarmed. "In a manner of speaking. I told him that I had never seen any 'prayer scrolls,' which I haven't. He then said he thought he accidentally overheard a Novice and me talking about them in the garden one morning. I told him I didn't know of a Novice who had any prayer scrolls either. He looked to be getting a little frustrated and described the specific morning in the garden where he had overheard us. I had to do some quick thinking now because he started pushing the issue concerning things he overheard. I finally told him we were discussing the boy's future service to God and what things he might learn from the examples of the Apostles. Which is all perfectly true in a sense."

"Did he believe you?" Jamisen asked.

"I think so. He made a little small talk and then left."

It was evident that Lohn was upset at his potential mistake, but everyone agreed that he had handled the encounter brilliantly. "At any rate, we cannot worry about what is done," interjected Mr. Estes. "I am agreed with Lohn. He has no true basis for believing we know anything about the scrolls or even their existence. It is a wonder in itself that he knows anything about them. We must continue on and leave today as planned."

With that, the four left to make final preparations. Clip had already packed his bag before breakfast, so he grabbed it and made for the south entrance to the abbey courtyard where they were to meet. There were some stone benches on either side of the gate that led to the main drive. Clip plopped his bag down on one of these and himself beside it. From here he had a view of almost all the courtyard. The activity was much the same as when he had arrived a couple of days before. People were milling around and talking or walking here and there at a patient pace. Many monks and students alike could be seen sitting on similar benches in the garden areas alone among shrubs or in a half concealed nook. It was a scene that seemed alive and thriving with life to Clip, but at the same time there was a sense of tranquility and community that Clip could sense just in the brief time he had spent there. He wondered if his college life for him would be similar.

Right now college seemed like a time and place far beyond Clip's reckoning. In retrospect, all the worry he had over picking a college seemed trivial when compared to what he was a part of now. How quickly God could open a door of purpose in one's life.

Clip was roused from his thought by the sight of Jamisen making his way across the courtyard. He was wearing loose fitting cargo pants with big pockets, a blue T-shirt and a cap with the school's insignia on it. He had a backpack, much like Clip's, hanging on one shoulder. He took long, quick strides, which made him stick out like a sore thumb in the scene Clip had been observing.

Jamisen noticed the bewildered look on Clip's face as he

approached. "Were you expecting someone else?" Jamisen said with a knowing grin.

"Where are your robes?"

"In my room."

"Are you allowed to dress like that?"

"Of course. There is no rule against wearing *civilian* clothes."

"Nice pack. Looks like you're traveling light, too."

"Mr. Estes sent an email to Lohn telling me what I should bring."

Lohn and Mr. Estes were making their way across the courtyard toward the two young men. "Well, are you ready for this?" Clip asked.

"Definitely."

"I see you boys are anxious to be off," Lohn said with a smile. He escorted the would-be adventurers to the main gate where a taxi waited for them. A few yards before they reached the gate, Lohn had Clip and Jamisen remove their hats and he placed his hands on their heads." Go with God. May His countenance shine upon you. May His strength uplift you. May His grace give you traveler's mercies on your journey. Above all, may your work benefit His Kingdom. Amen."

Clip felt empowered after Lohn's prayer. He felt the weight of the moment and the task at hand. Jamisen and Clip said their goodbyes to Lohn, and loaded into the taxi. Mr. Estes had a few private words with Lohn before he joined them. Lohn stuck his head in the window of the taxi and said, "You boys take care of this old man." With that admonition, he smacked the top of the taxi a couple of times, and it sped away. Clip could see Lohn standing in the road waving until they were out of sight.

The taxi took them to the bus station in the village. They then took the bus to Leeds, where they took a final taxi to the airport. A connecting flight to London was required, and then they were off to Beijing.

They rode in first class, which seemed to make Mr.

Estes feel uncomfortable again, but Clip and Jamisen ate it up. Jamisen was in wide-eyed wonder. He had never traveled further than a hundred miles from Stansberry, and those times had been few and far between. He was soaking up everything he saw and every new experience no matter how minute.

It was not long before Mr. Estes was napping in his seat across the aisle from Clip and Jamisen. The two had been talking nonstop since they boarded the plane. Nothing about the scrolls was mentioned. The journey itself was taking on an adventurous mystique that had them almost giddy. Jamisen had borrowed a book about China from the abbey library and he and Clip were pouring over it and discussing the culture.

Talk soon turned to Clip's home and what it was like where he lived. Jamisen sat in rapt attention as Clip described his town, family, and past experiences growing up. This was one of the things Clip really liked about Jamisen. He was a great listener. Many people Clip had known heard what you said, but never seemed like they were expending too much energy actually listening and processing it. Jamisen always listened as if he had a vested interest in what was being said.

After a while, Clip turned the conversation in a different direction. "How did you get permission to come?" Clip asked curiously. He was not familiar at all with the Benedictine way of life, but he was sure Jamisen had some restrictions placed on him as a Novice.

"Mr. Estes asked the abbot if I could escort him on a mission trip to Asia. He said it would be a growing experience for me and reaffirm my commitment of service to God."

Clip was quiet for a moment, and then asked the question that had been nagging at him ever since he met Jamisen. "What made you decide to become a monk?"

"I've been wondering when you were going to ask me that."

Clip looked mildly perplexed. "It's just that when I hear the word *monk*, I always pictured a little bald-headed old man who doesn't want to be around people. I now know that I've got the people part wrong, but I didn't realize that young people could become one."

Jamisen laughed. "Most people who haven't met a monk or visited an abbey think that way. You do have to be eighteen to first apply as a novice. I turned eighteen six months ago, and I took the first step the day of my birthday. Although I have known for a long time now this is what I want to do with my life."

"I think it's a great calling, but how do you give up . . . well, all the stuff you have to give up?

"You mean like, girls?"

Clip grinned. "Well, yeah."

"I haven't told you before, but I was an orphan. I grew up in the Children's Home in the village outside of Stansberry. The brothers and priests from the abbey were constantly doing things for us like Christmas parties and making sure we had a present on our birthday. They organized athletic teams, and they often had picnics and games for us in the fields surrounding the abbey. I grew up in their kindness. Lohn took me under his wing many years ago and has been like a father to me. When I got old enough to start thinking about what I wanted to do with my life, I knew from the beginning I wanted to be a part of something committed to service and committed to God."

Clip felt like a spoiled brat with the commitment of a jellyfish. Jamisen saw the look on his face. "Hey, it's not for everybody. And, don't think I don't wonder about what I might have done or become if I had chosen another vocation, but when it comes down to it, I am very happy with my decision. The job does have its strong points."

"Such as?"

"I'm already getting to travel with a hillbilly from the states and millionaire."

They both laughed and spent the rest of the flight napping and watching in-flight movies.

Chapter 8

Their plane arrived in Beijing in the late afternoon. Mr. Estes, Clip, and Jamisen made their way through customs and to the baggage claim. While they were waiting for their bags to arrive, Clip heard a voice hollering across the baggage carousel. "Roff! Roff! Hello!"

An older looking Chinese man was waving and gesturing in their direction. "Is he talking to us?" Clip asked.

Mr. Estes looked up. "Oh, wonderful. It's Abraham."

Abraham seemed like an odd name to Clip for a Chinese man. He looked at Jamisen, and he seemed to be thinking the same thing.

"Roff. Hello. Good to see you again. I receive your instructions by the email day before yesterday. All is O.K." The old man grinned from ear to ear.

"Good. It is wonderful to see you as well, Abraham, but I didn't expect you to come yourself. May I introduce my friends, Clip and Jamisen."

Abraham shook both their hands vigorously. "Happy to meet you. Roff tell me about you on phone. You are good boys."

Both boys grinned and were instantly taken with the old man. The boys learned that Abraham was an old friend of Mr. Estes' that he had sold boats to for many years. He ran a lake resort for government officials in Kunming, a large city in the southern part of China. Mr. Estes had contacted him and asked if he could make arrangements for their time in China. Abraham had come personally to see to their needs.

He hailed a taxi for them, and it was all he could do to load Jamisen and Clip into it for all their gawking at their surroundings. Abraham had made hotel arrangements for the men and as the taxi made it's way to the hotel Jamisen and Clip were plastered to the windows trying to grasp every image as the taxi whipped through the busy streets of Beijing. Abraham was turned around in the passenger's seat trying to point out things of interest, but the mass of buildings and people was 'sensory overload' for the two young men and they retained nothing much of what Abraham said.

When they arrived at the hotel, Abraham instructed them to wash-up and rest while he made preparations for dinner. Clip and Jamisen shared a room, and Mr. Estes had his own room. The boys each showered the stickiness of travel off of them and changed clothes, but because they were both still riding the adrenaline high of being immersed in a foreign country, resting was out of the question. After about and hour, Abraham came knocking at the door. He and Mr. Estes were waiting in the hall.

"OK, we go now to eat," Abraham said enthusiastically. "We have traditional Chinese food tonight. Not like American Chinese restaurant. All authentic. Good time. Good ferrowship."

Abraham led them down the bustling streets. Clip was amazed at the ebb and flow of the many people, cars, and bicycles beyond count that moved in a kind of placated harmony. Yes, there was a lot of horn blowing and the constant ringing of bicycle bells, but all moved with understanding. One unusual thing Clip noticed right away was that the lanky Jamisen was taller than any Chinese person he had seen so far. Jamisen was keenly aware of this as well and walked with his head up like a farmer walking through a wheat field.

Another observation Clip made was the smell. It wasn't a bad smell. It was just a *different* kind of smell. It was a cultural smell. The many street-side restaurants, millions of car exhaust fumes, poorly drained gutters, steam vents, and many other things Clip was not familiar with, combined to form a tangy, leaden smell that permeated everything.

After a few blocks, Abraham stopped at what looked like

an entrance to a pet shop. Inside the door were many aquariums, large buckets, and even plastic garbage cans filled with all manor of sea life. There were fish of varying sizes and species, turtles, eels, shrimp, clams, and some things neither Clip nor Jamisen recognized. Abraham left them standing in the doorway while he went and inspected the holding tanks. He pointed to several things as a man who worked in the restaurant wrote down his choices. The group was then led through the main dining area to a private room in the back. They were seated at a very large, round table that had the biggest 'lazy-susan' turntable Clip had ever seen.

The turntable was already laden with food of various kinds. There were four or five plates of vegetables that were fried or boiled, small strips of pork served cold, peanuts, bean curd, watermelon slices, and of course rice. Placed in front of them were a small bowl and plate, chopsticks, and a soupspoon.

"Please, begin. Begin," Abraham said enthusiastically as he began to pour everyone what looked like Coke to drink.

The boys did not really know how to start, so they followed Mr. Estes' lead. He used his chopsticks to take a small portion of food from some of the dishes on the turntable. He used his chopsticks with the skill of a veteran. Jamisen and Clip tried to follow suit, but more food ended up on the table than in their plates. Abraham and Mr. Estes laughed good-heartedly at their attempts. Clip almost lost an eye in Jamisen's attempt to grasp a peanut with his chopsticks. The would-be-missile squirted out of the chopsticks and made a direct hit on his eye before he had a chance to react. All of them got a good kick out of it, including Clip.

The food then started coming in courses. The seafood Abraham picked came out on steaming hot plates that smelled delicious but didn't always look appealing to the western eyes of Jamisen and Clip. They managed to pick, stab, and grab enough food during the hour-long meal to satisfy them nicely. Abraham had been right when he said that it was not like Chinese restaurants back home. The highlight of the meal though was dessert. The waitress brought out a steaming hot plate that had little gooey balls heaped in a great pile.

"Eat quickly," Abraham instructed as he nabbed two of the golf ball size treats and dipped them in a little bowl of water that had been brought with the dish.

Jamisen and Clip did as they were told with a little apprehension, but they were pleasantly surprised. The inside of the ball was banana that had been fried and covered with a sweet caramel like sauce. When they dipped the ball into the water, the sticky sauce hardened into a shell. The boys understood why they needed to hurry after a few minutes. Once the sauce cooled, it was impossible to pull the balls off the serving dish on which they were brought.

After what turned out to be a very satisfying first meal in China, the four made their way leisurely back to the hotel. Neither Jamisen nor Clip spoke on the way back. Both were absorbed in the night sights and sounds of one of the world's largest and most populated cities.

Abraham saw them to their rooms and then retired to his. After a few minutes, Mr. Estes came to Jamisen and Clip's room to discuss their next steps. Abraham had arranged for transport on a train to Xi'an the next day. Mr. Estes said that the boys should enjoy it because it was the best way to see the country.

"Is Abraham a Christian?" Clip asked thinking he already knew the answer.

"No, he is not," Mr. Estes replied.

Jamisen and Clip both raised their eyebrows in surprise. "But he seems so . . . nice," Clip said unsure of how to word his thoughts.

"Ah. Do you think all nice people are Christians, Clip?" Mr. Estes asked with a chuckle.

"No, but he is one of your friends, and he seems so genuine," Clip said defensively.

"You are correct on both accounts. He is my friend of

many years, and he is a genuine person. The goodness Abraham offers is straight from his heart, but he is not a Christian," Mr. Estes said with more seriousness. "I have of course tried to witness to him many, many times. Even his name was given to him by a missionary that lived in his village when he was a boy. His real name is Li Phu. He wanted a western name also, so of course the missionary gave him a Biblical name. But you will find there are many good people in this world who live by a code of ethics and morality that aligns perfectly with the Bible, but they choose not to accept the salvation that is offered by God. Abraham is one of these. He is one of the most honest and compassionate men I have ever known, but I know that if he does not accept Jesus as his Lord and Savior, I will not see him in Heaven. It is a burden I carry every time we part."

It bothered Clip to think a man as nice as Abraham would not be going to Heaven. Abraham was obviously a smart man by his elevated position, and he was a man of good moral integrity. So why would he not accept a God who upheld his way of life? It was a problem Clip would wrestle with many other times during his life.

After discussing travel arrangements for the next day, Mr. Estes left them for the night to ponder the day's events. They talked about the food they had eaten, and they talked about what they had seen of the city.

The next morning Abraham was waiting for them in the lobby. "Good morning," he said with his infectious smile. "OK. We get breakfast first. Then go to train station by nine o'clock."

Jamisen, Clip, and Mr. Estes hoisted their packs, and Clip also carried Mr. Estes' briefcase that held his laptop which contained the scroll information. Abraham carried a small duffle bag that held his belongings. He guided them to another hole-in-the wall restaurant for breakfast. It was bustling with customers who gave the foreigners only a cursory glance. The site of foreigners in Beijing was a common occurrence in these days. The appearance of a Caucasian did not elicit the stares it once did only a few years prior.

The meal was strange to Jamisen and Clip in that it was more like a meal they would have at lunch or supper at their homes. There was rice again and vegetables. There was a bitter clear soup, boiled eggs that had to be peeled, and dumplings. They were treated once again though by a dessert of sorts. One of the servings was a plate of doughy rolls that appeared to have not been baked completely. These were for dipping in a sweet, white sauce like icing except much thinner. The boys engorged themselves on the rolls. They both felt foolish though for expecting breakfast to be something like bacon, eggs, and French toast.

Another taxi transported them to the train station. Clip got car sick in the short time they were actually in the car. The weaving and sudden stopping and starting took a toll on him. Jamisen acted as if he was on a ride at an amusement park. His commentary and "Wheeee's" did nothing to ease Clip's stomach.

The train station was a hub of activity. There did not seem to be the slightest bit of order to the chaos that reigned. There were no lines or ordered boarding protocol. There were just masses of people worming their way onto one train or the other, sometimes while other masses were worming their way off a train.

Jamisen and Clip had a decided advantage in their height. They could see where to go much easier than Mr. Estes and Abraham could, but since neither one could read Chinese, they had to let Abraham lead the way to their train. He had bought the tickets the day before, so it was just a matter of finding the right train.

Abraham found it without any trouble. They boarded and were directed to a small cabin in one of the cars. The cabin had four bunk beds that went up one side and four that went up the other side. There were no other chairs in the room, only a small corner storage area for baggage and a window with shabby curtains.

Abraham seemed very pleased with the cabin, and Clip and Jamisen soon learned why. Once the train started, Abraham led them to a sitting car. As they walked through the train, they saw people packed into the small cabins with people occupying all the bunks. The occupants were also forced to store their luggage on the bunk with them or out in the hallway because of the inadequate space for cargo. They soon discovered Abraham had bought the other four bunk spaces so that they could have privacy.

The sitting car was filling up quickly with people who could not stand the suffocating cabins. The car was dirty, as was most of the train, and held very simple furnishings. There were rows of booths positioned back-to-back on both sides of the car. Some had tables between the seats, but most did not. Abraham found them a booth where the four of them could sit together. It was a tight fit because they had brought their luggage with them at the urging of Abraham.

The train rolled at what seemed a slow pace to Jamisen and Clip who had both ridden trains in their respective countries. Clip estimated it was moving at about forty-five miles an hour. "How long will it take us to get to Xi'an?" he asked Abraham.

"About twenty hour because the train will make many stops."

They were soon out of the city, and the Chinese countryside was rolling past their eyes. In a matter of minutes, the boys felt transported back in time. It was surreal to see the primitive farms and even more primitive homes after leaving one of the largest cities on the planet. At times, there were rice paddies as far as the eye could see, then a village would spring from the horizon boasting squat, brick homes. Often these homes had no glass in the windows, just plastic coverings or nothing at all.

Many of the villages had pearl farms. This was a new concept to the boys that had to be explained by Abraham. They had both noticed small ponds dotting the outskirts of many of the villages they passed. Floating in these ponds were dozens and sometimes hundreds of plastic drink bottles. Abraham explained these were pearl farms. The bottles marked the location of where the artificial pearls were being grown.

They passed through flat, open regions at times, and then a hilly, sometimes mountainous region would arise. As the countryside passed their eyes, Jamisen and Clip both became more comfortable in their role as world travelers. Lunch came in the form of a steaming hot soup that was very spicy. There were no spoons, so they drank straight from the bowl.

They talked the hours and miles away. Mr. Estes spoke of some of his experiences while doing business in China, but Jamisen and Clip were fascinated by the stories Abraham told of his life. Abraham had survived the Cultural Revolution, a dark time in the history of China. He was now part of the growing citizenry that embraced the West with its technology and social norms.

He said at one point, "You know, the most sought after teacher at the universities in China are native speakers of Engrish. These people who come from America, Engrand, and Australia are treated like superstar on the campuses. Everybody want to learn Engrish. Everybody want to have Western style. Especially the young peoples. They are still limited in their freedom, but they have much more freedom than my generation. They embrace the West, and I think it is good for them. We can still honor our culture while moving into the future, but many people in our government do not see it that way."

Later Mr. Estes told the boys that it was very subversive for Abraham to talk the way he had, and that twenty years ago he might have been killed for it if any government official heard him.

Supper was several kabobs that contained pork and hot tea to drink. When it was too dark to see out the windows, they headed back to the cabin and turned in for the night. The beds turned out to be perfectly sized for Chinese people, but Jamisen and Clip had a more difficult time. Neither one could stretch out their legs completely. It was a bed though, for some people on the train had to sit in the hard booths all the way to Xi'an. Clip spent a few moments writing in his journal he had brought along, and then he joined the others in sleep.

CHAPTER 9

Xi'an seemed a large city to Clip. Not anywhere near the size of Beijing, but it is still very large. The book Jamisen had brought on the trip said that it was one of the oldest cities in China, and that it was the capital city of many of China's early dynasties. According to the book, Xi'an once rivaled Rome and Constantinople as the greatest city in the world.

As their train neared the city, Clip noticed a large airport just outside it. "There's an airport. Why didn't we fly here?" he asked Mr. Estes.

"I wanted you and Jamisen to get to see some of the country, and the train is the best way to do that. Besides, I have waited fifteen years for this trip. A day or two longer won't hurt anything."

Abraham arranged for a taxi to take them to a hotel and one to take him to the airport. He was returning to Kunming, so he said a tearful goodbye to Mr. Estes. Both men knew it would probably be the last time they would see the other because they were both getting older and had other responsibilities. "Abraham, my good friend, it was an honor to have you bring us to our destination. I owe you a big one."

"The honor was mine, Roff. You have been a good friend to me for many year. I only wish I could have done more. Goodbye and good ruck to you. And good ruck to you," he said turning to Jamisen and Clip. "It was preasure meeting you. You take care. Grow up, and be like Roff." And with that he hopped in his taxi and was gone.

Even though he had only known the man for a short time, Clip felt sad at the parting. He also wondered how Mr.

Estes must be feeling after knowing he probably said goodbye to a friend he would never see in Heaven.

The taxi took the three of them to a nice hotel, even nicer than the one they stayed in while in Beijing. They went to their rooms with Jamisen and Clip sharing a room again. Mr. Estes suggested they all clean up and rest for a while. They could meet together in his room in a few hours. That sounded great to the boys, who felt more than a little tired after fitful sleep in the small bunks.

After showering, the boys took a nap for a couple of hours. They then amused themselves by flipping through the television channels and watching the various Chinese programs. After a while, Mr. Estes rang them on the phone, and they went to his room to discuss their next move.

Mr. Estes took out his laptop and turned it on. He had to use the thumbprint security scanner to access his files. Displayed on it was a map of Xi'an and the surrounding area. "OK, boys. Take a look. Here we are." He pointed to a section on the northeast side of town. "And here is the spot we will be heading for—Louguan, it is a town about fifty miles southwest of the city. The Daqin Pagoda is near Louguan. We will take a taxi there for simplicity's sake. It shouldn't take more than an hour and a half if the roads are good. Once we reach the town, we will find a place to stay and then visit the sight of the church. From there, your guess is as good as mine. We will have to 'play it by ear' and hope we find some clues."

"What about the last line in the clues, the one about 'treading like fish'?" Jamisen asked.

Mr. Estes clicked a few times with the mouse and pulled up the coded directions. He read the last line out loud: *"Tread 300 in the way of the fish.* Again, your guess is as good as mine. Lohn and I have tried in vain to come up with an answer and have been unsuccessful. Hopefully, with the Lord's help, an answer will present itself. For now, why don't we get something to eat? I suggest we take our packs and the briefcase. Foreign visitors are sometimes the target of theft in these large cities."

The three companions made their way down to the hotel restaurant. Their waiter did not speak English at all, but the restaurant manager spoke enough to understand they would eat whatever dishes were brought. The food was similar to what they had in Beijing, except there were more small dishes of pork and chicken rather than seafood.

Jamisen noticed three Caucasian men eating at a corner table. It caught his attention because they were the first they had seen since arriving in Beijing. They were dressed in casual clothes and seemed not to have noticed Mr. Estes,' Clip's, and Jamisen's presence in the dining room. He pointed it out to Clip and Mr. Estes, but the men were soon forgotten as the talk turned back to the scrolls.

After the meal, they wandered a few blocks to the east and then to the west of the hotel, more to stretch their legs than sightseeing of any kind. The mystery of the scrolls had taken hold of all three of them to a great extent now that they were so close to finding one. They discussed what the last line in the directions could mean, what kind of container the scroll might be in, and whether or not it would be legible after all these years.

They returned to the hotel and found the three Caucasian men sitting in the lobby. The tallest member of the group rose from his seat and approached Mr. Estes. He had an athletic build, short brown hair, and piercing blue eyes. He smiled at Mr. Estes and extended his hand. "Mr. Ralph Estes?" he said in American English.

"Yes. How may I help you?"

"My name is Jason Bell. My employer would very much like to meet with you if you have time this evening."

"Really? And who is your employer?"

"I am sorry, but I am not at liberty to say. But he says to tell you it is very important he speak with you. Will you come to his room?"

Mr. Estes did not reply for a moment. Then he said, "I would feel more comfortable meeting in the lounge . . . say in fifteen minutes?"

"Very well. I will tell him."

With that, the man and his two companions left. Mr. Estes and the boys went to the lounge. It was practically empty except for a few people at the bar. They went to the back of the room opposite the bar and sat at a table that was partially isolated by a foldable screen.

"Who do you think it is, and what does he want?" Clip asked.

"I have no idea. But I don't think I'm going to like it."

"I've got a bad feeling about this, also. I think we should leave," Jamisen said rising.

Mr. Estes shook his head. "No. It is better to see a villain face to face than face a thief in the night. Let's see who it is and what they want."

A waitress came over and they ordered some hot tea. In a few moments they saw Bell leading the two other men into the lounge, and a smaller man followed them. He was obscured by the other three. The group approached the table, and the three men parted to let the smaller man through. Mr. Estes let out a small gasp. It was Bishop Sorlenni.

"Hello, gentlemen. It is good to finally meet you. I am sorry we never got a chance to talk at the abbey, but you left before we had the opportunity," Sorlenni said in his lilting Italian accent.

Clip was not sure how the others felt, but the sight of the bishop surrounded by what looked like henchmen made him very nervous. A glance at Jamisen showed he felt the same way. Mr. Estes' face belayed no emotion. He was looking the bishop straight in the eye.

"Well, now we have the opportunity, Bishop Sorlenni. Won't you sit down?" Mr. Estes said as if he were conducting a business meeting. If he was nervous, he was not showing it.

"Thank you. But please, call me Dominique. May I call you Ralph?"

"Of course."

The bishop sat down, along with Bell and the other two men. "You have met my associate, Mr. Bell already. This is Mr. Rollins," he pointed to the broad shouldered man with a flat top haircut sitting at his left. "And this is Mr. Danner," he said pointing to short, stocky man with bleached blond hair sitting at his right.

"Are you also priests?" asked Mr. Estes.

The bishop smiled. "No. But they do work for me."

"What is it you want?" Mr. Estes asked matter-of-factly.

"I want to know if you are seeking the Prayer Scrolls of the Apostles."

"You already know the answer to that, or you would not be here," said Mr. Estes without missing a step or blinking.

"I was hoping we could share our knowledge and work together to find them."

"You have no knowledge, or you wouldn't be talking to me."

"We know more than you think, but you are right. There are several key parts of the puzzle that we do not have."

"When you say *we,* are you referring to the Vatican?"

"The Vatican does not officially support the finding of the scrolls, for they are out of the memory of many, and their existence is not known to most. And of those who do know of them, few believe in their power. I am one of those few who serve the Church and know of their existence and the power they hold."

"So that is what you are seeking . . . power?"

"To be quite honest, yes, in a way. We do seek power, but power for the good of the Church. You will agree we live in a world that does not acknowledge the authority of the Church as it once did. The Prayer Scrolls offer an opportunity to reignite the flame of influence we once carried. I have learned much about you, Mr. Estes. I know that you are a believer and servant of God, so our goals are the same."

"That is where you are wrong," Mr. Estes said with touch of anger. "The scrolls were not meant to glorify the Church or any other earthly entity or person. They were meant to glorify God and his works alone. You are no different than the priests of old who tried to use the scrolls for personal power and gain."

"What will you do with the scrolls if you were to find them then, Mr. Estes? What is your selfless grand design?"

"We will use them as they were meant to be used, to help a world in need, as was God's will."

"So you claim to know God's will. You feel you have the knowledge and right to wield the power of the scrolls. Surely you must know the scrolls were meant to be kept by true ordained men of God and used at *their* discretion."

"If your intentions were as pure as you claimed, you would know that the scrolls were not meant to be kept by anyone but to be used to touch a world that has forgotten the power of God."

"Do you not think it was providence, Mr. Estes, that placed me at the abbey and allowed me to overhear your friends discussing the scrolls. I am one of a handful of people who even know about them or even believe in them still. Do you think this a coincidence?"

Mr. Estes looked contemplative for a moment, and Clip was afraid he was going to relent. "No. I don't think it was coincidence. I think the devil works in many ways to usurp the Kingdom of God."

At this statement, the bishop's visage became stony and his face flushed. "I had hoped we might work together to find the scrolls, but I see now that our opinions differ greatly as to their proper place within the Church."

"Well, I am sorry you traveled so far to only be disappointed, for we will not aid you in turning the scrolls into a religious pawn. Jamisen. Clip. We are leaving now."

Mr. Estes and the boys shouldered their bags and made to leave. The bishop put out his hand and stopped Mr. Estes as he started past. "I may not be as disappointed as you think, Mr. Estes. Our paths may cross yet again."

Clip grabbed the bishop's hand and removed it less than gently. "That might not be in your best interests, sir."

Bell chuckled at this, but they took no more action to hamper their leaving. The boys followed Mr. Estes who was walking quickly now that they were out of the lounge. They took the elevator to their rooms on the third floor.

"Listen to me carefully, boys. I'm afraid our situation has become dangerous. I don't like the look of those men Sorlenni had with him. I want you to gather your things as quickly as possible and meet me in my room. Obviously, Lohn and I have been much too careless. We are going to have to try and get out of the hotel without them seeing us, and then we will decide what to do from there."

Jamisen and Clip did not like the sound in Mr. Estes' voice when making that last statement, but neither said anything as they hurried to their room to collect the few things they did not already have in their packs. It only took a minute, and they peered down the hall before exiting their rooms but saw no signs of anyone watching. They hurried across to Mr. Estes' room. He was packed as well and was standing by the window looking out.

"We may have caught a lucky break," he said motioning them to the window. "There is a fire escape outside here, but there seems to be no way to open the window. I suppose if it were an emergency, they expect people to just break the window. It must be a safety measure to keep people from being able to climb up and enter rooms from outside."

"Well, this seems like an emergency to me," said Jamisen eyeing the room for something to break the window with.

"You are probably right," said Mr. Estes. "But we have

to do it without drawing attention, and without making much noise.

"I've got an idea!" Clip offered excitedly. "I saw this thing on TV once where car thieves broke into cars using a spark plug to break a side window. They tapped the window with the spark plug until a spidery crack formed all over it. Then they pushed the window in without any noise."

"OK. It's worth a shot. Look for something with a hard, sharp point."

They began searching the room for something they could use. Clip mourned the fact he was not able to bring his pocketknife. "Hey, what about this?" Jamisen asked as he came from his search in the bathroom. It was about and eight inch metal rod that was used as a part of a lever inside the toilet bowl tank.

Clip took it and felt the weight in his hands. "This should work."

He took the rod and began tapping the window. It made more noise than he had anticipated, so he stopped after several tries. He looked at Mr. Estes and Jamisen for guidance.

"What do you think?"

"Maybe if you gave it one swift tap you could begin the break," Mr. Estes answered. "But, I think you will need something to hit it with."

Once again Jamisen came to the rescue. He picked up the stainless steel hot water thermos that was in the room for tea. "OK. You hold the rod, Clip, and I'll give it a go," he said taking practice jabs with the bottom end of the thermos.

"OK. Just make sure you hit it square."

Clip placed the rod against the window and held it firmly with both hands. Jamisen hit it with the bottom end of the thermos, but nothing happened other than producing a loud dinging sound.

"You are going to have to hit it harder," said Clip.

Jamisen reared back this time and gave it a hard lick. Still nothing happened. "Harder," Clip said again.

Jamisen took the thermos in both hands and gave the rod a swift, hard blow. The window cracked this time, but not as Clip had planned. A large chunk of the window broke into a thousand pieces and fell to the alley below, where it made a good bit of noise.

The three of them stood frozen. Clip peered out the window to see if the noise had drawn any attention, but all he could hear was the night traffic of Xi'an.

"Well, I think there is too much noise coming from the street for anybody to have heard, and nobody is in the alley."

"Smashing job, Clip! No pun intended," said Jamisen with a wry smile.

They used the thermos and rod to chip away at the edges of the glass. This way they made little noise, and less force was required. It took only few minutes to get an opening large enough for them to comfortably fit through.

Clip double checked the alley for signs of life then started to go through.

"Wait," said Mr. Estes. He ran to the small desk in the room and pulled out an envelope with the hotel insignia on it. He took several hundred U.S. dollars worth of Chinese money and put it in the envelope, along with a note apologizing for the window. He wrote *Hotel Manager* on the outside and sealed it.

"I don't know if he or the maid will end up with it, but I will feel better knowing I tried."

With that, they crept out the window and down the fire escape. The first two levels they went down were stairs with rails, but the last level was a rusty ladder attached to two heavy springs. The ladder let down with the weight of the person. Clip was the first down. As soon as he stepped on the ladder, it released smoothly down to the alley. He climbed down, and landed with a short jump on the paved surface. Jamisen climbed down a little more precariously as he had to carry Mr. Estes' briefcase. He also landed with a jump and began scanning the alley and the street for any trouble.

It was slower going for Mr. Estes, but Clip was impressed with his mobility. He made a little hop off the ladder that sent it shooting back up to its resting place. Mr. Estes stumbled backward a little after his hop but Clip caught hold of his backpack and steadied him.

"Thank you, Clip. I can't escape from Chinese hotels as nimbly as I used to," he said with a laugh.

"Now what?" asked Jamisen.

"We find a taxi and get across town to another hotel first," answered Mr. Estes.

They followed the alley to the backside of the hotel and then made their way down the street as quickly as they could. After two blocks, they were able to hail a taxi. Mr. Estes tried in vain to explain to the driver they wanted a hotel across town. The driver finally acknowledged with: "Hotel. OK. Hotel. Yes."

They drove around for probably ten minutes before the taxi pulled up in front of the hotel from which they had just escaped.

"No! No!" said Mr. Estes in agitation. "Go on. Go on."

The driver pulled back into traffic. He obviously thought he had some foolish foreigners, and that he could make some easy money back circling around to the hotel they were a couple blocks from.

Jamisen pulled out a map of the city that was on the back of one of the hotel brochures he had picked up that morning. It was in Chinese, but finally through much pointing and gesturing, he made the taxi driver understand they wanted to be taken across town. This time the taxi driver came through for them and took them almost to the city limits on the west side.

He stopped in front of a hotel that looked a little worse than the one they had just left. Mr. Estes paid the fair but gave no tip for his attempt at gouging them. At the check-in desk, Mr. Estes gave a false name, and when he was asked to produce his passport, 200 Yuan, or the equivalent of about twenty-five dollars, made the requirement slip the mind of the desk attendant.

Mr. Estes booked a room with two beds. He did not feel comfortable leaving the boys alone after the day's events. Their room was on the first floor, a point that was not lost on Jamisen or Clip. As soon as they entered, Mr. Estes made a beeline for the phone.

"I must call Lohn and tell him what has happened, then we will figure out how we are going to get out of the city tomorrow."

The statement hit both boys like a hammer. "Get out of the city! Why are we getting out of the city? We are not going to let those guys scare us are we?" Clip said with a little more hostility than he meant.

"It's not safe. I could see the look in the bishop's eyes. He will stop at nothing to get the scrolls, and he will feel justified in doing whatever he does in the name of the Church, even if the Church is not sanctioning it."

Jamisen and Clip both looked crushed. "I am sorry, boys. But, I will not risk your lives for the scrolls. It boils down to the fact that Lohn and I were much too careless in this endeavor. I guess we assumed we were on a holy mission that would not be noticed by the world."

"But it *is* a holy mission," Clip argued. "If we don't find the scrolls, someone like the bishop might. We can't give up now. Jamisen and I are not afraid." He looked at Jamisen for support.

He nodded his head. "Clip is right. If we don't do it, who will?"

"I'm sorry, but we can't worry about that right now. I won't put you two at risk for an old man's dream. Now, I must call Lohn and see what is to be done."

He picked up the old phone and dialed the number to the abbey. It was early morning at Stansberry. Lohn had just risen and was starting his morning prayers. "Hello, Lohn. It's Ralph . . . fine, but I'm afraid I have some bad news. We arrived in Xi'an today and were met by Bishop Sorlenni and three very unsavory looking men who work for him . . . yes, apparently he followed us or knew of our coming . . . yes, he new about them. He wanted us to work with them in finding them . . . no, I think for the moment we gave them the slip. We are at a different hotel now across town. Do you have any suggestions for getting out of the city? No, not to go to Louguan. To come back to Stansberry . . . I don't agree, Lohn. They are at risk . . . yes, I know that, but I think Sorlenni will stop at nothing to get the scrolls. Look how he was able to track us down so easily . . . I know we weren't careful, but that is our fault . . . but . . . yes . . . I suppose you are right. I know they are . . . O.K. . . . if I hadn't been with them the whole time, I would have accused them of calling you first. Very well . . . thank you. We will need it. Goodbye.

"Well, it looks like Lohn is in your corner. He thinks we should move ahead as planned with much added caution."

"Brilliant!" said Jamisen bursting into a grin.

"Let's get some sleep. I don't know about you boys, but all this 'cloak and dagger' stuff has exhausted me. Tomorrow will be a long day, and we need to be fresh."

All three slept until well after lunch. They did not eat in the hotel restaurant for fear of making themselves conspicuous. Jamisen tried to order room service over the phone, but gave up after several attempts. Mr. Estes paid their bill, and they left the hotel on an empty stomach. There was a line of taxis parked in front of the hotel waiting on a fare, so they had no trouble finding one.

They hoppped in the first one in line, and Jamisen used a map from the book on China he brought to show the driver where they wanted to go. He shook his head no several times and kept spreading his arms apart while hammering the companions with Chinese. They finally understood that he thought the distance was too far, so they exited his taxi and tried the next one in line. This produced the same results, but after Mr. Estes handed him several hundred Yuan, he nodded his agreement.

The roads were in decent shape, so the going was pretty

fast. It took about an hour and a half as Mr. Estes predicted. The trip offered the boys another chance to become momentarily immersed in the Chinese landscape. Though the scenery was much the same as when they rode the train, it was still a spectacular experience for Jamisen and Clip.

Louguan was a very small city in comparison to Xi'an and Beijing, but it is still afforded many modern accommodations. They had no trouble finding a suitable hotel, and they once again reserved just one room. Mr. Estes suggested they not waste a moment and head straight for the Daqin Pagoda near Mount Zohngnan, so they took their bags and Mr. Estes' briefcase and left the hotel without even seeing their room.

As it turned out, it was not at all hard to find. There were tourist brochures in the lobby of the hotel, for it seemed that Mount Zhongnan with its many Taoist temples was one of the main attractions near the town.

It was easy enough to get a taxi there after showing the driver the brochure. The ride took less than a half hour outside of town to a wooded and mountainous region. The brochure had an English side, so Jamisen read it to them as they rode. They soon learned that not only were there Taoist temples there, but it was actually the founding site of Taoism. Mr. Estes knew this, but had never mentioned it. "It doesn't say anything about the Daqin pagoda or anything about an early Christian church," Jamisen said scanning the brochure once more.

"I doubt you will find any information regarding it when we get there either," Mr. Estes replied. "We will recognize it by its structure though. From what I have read, it has seven stories and is leaning very precariously ever since an earthquake in 1556. No one had entered it until the British historian discovered its roots. There is supposed to be a rebuilding project in progress to repair and update the structure. We will just have to see when we get there."

All three of the companions were getting very excited and nervous with anticipation. Mr. Estes kept drumming his fingers on his knee and humming bits of tunes. Jamisen and Clip kept craning their necks first one way then another to try and get an early glimpse of their destination. Mount Zohngnan turned out to be a small mountain covered with ancient temples and overlook terraces. Open fields with clumps of trees and rocky protrusions surrounded the mountain in a patchwork of layered architecture.

Mr. Estes bought admission passes to visit the tourist area located on the mountain. Jamisen and Clip thought this a ridiculous operation, for there was only a small stone wall that ran a couple hundred yards in either direction of the main entrance to the mountain paths. With a little effort, someone could walk around the wall and not have to pay admission, but they soon learned that in order to enter any of the temples or buildings located on the mountain you had to have an admission ticket.

Before heading up the mountain, they bought some soup and spring rolls from a vendor for their first meal of the day. With no real idea of where to look for the Daqin pagoda, they started walking up the main path leading up the mountain. There were twisting, winding sets of stairs connected by well-maintained pathways. They walked back and forth on these paths until they reached the top of the mountain, but they had seen no sign of the Daqin.

The top of the mountain offered a panoramic view of the surrounding area. To the north, Louguan could be seen distantly through the haze. In all other directions, a green blanket of trees was all that could be seen. Mount Zohngnan was obviously a remote sight. Small buildings and pathways within a half mile of the mountain's base was all that broke up the forest for miles.

Clip had wandered to the southwest side of the vantage point and was scanning the forest below. "Hey! Come here and take a look at this."

Jamisen and Mr. Estes hurried over to where he stood peering down the side of the mountain. "There, past that line of trees about 200 yards below us. Do you see that?" he asked pointing down below.

Sticking up awkwardly high above the trees was the roof of a pagoda that was leaning to one side. "That has to be it!" said Jamisen, unable to mask the excitement in his voice.

Mr. Estes squinted at the crooked protrusion and said, "I believe you are right. Let's see if we can make our way down to it."

They picked a trail in the direction of the pagoda, sometimes using the path and sometimes walking through areas choked with foliage. After they had descended a little way, they came across a path leading in the direction of the pagoda. After a sharp turn past a rock outcropping, the ancient, seven-story temple loomed in front of them.

There was scaffolding surrounding the temple half way up, and there were tools and building materials scattered around the base. A small rope fence cordoned off the area to keep people out of the work site. The rebuilding of the structure was obviously still underway.

It had grown dusky dark during their descent down the mountain, and the workday had ended for the workmen who had been there. All three crept cautiously toward the leaning pagoda. They made a few circles around, just scanning the exterior. It was easy to tell that it was centuries old, but it somehow seemed rooted and strong, even with its lean. There was only one door that led into the temple. It was almost eight feet tall and was made of heavy wood.

Mr. Estes inspected the door. There was a lock clasped tightly shut. "Hmm. Well, it appears we are temporarily out of business."

"I can break the lock with one of these metal bars," Clip said picking up a three-foot long iron rod that was part of the construction material. "There's nobody around."

"Yes, I suppose you could," Mr. Estes said contemplating their situation. "But, I propose another idea. What say we go back to the hotel tonight, and tomorrow we can get some supplies to aid us in our investigation. We can get some food and drinks, and return tomorrow evening. We can spend the night searching the temple, when the likelihood of anyone catching us will be the least. Today is Friday, so there will probably not be any workmen there tomorrow or the next day since it is the weekend."

That sounded good to Jamisen and Clip, though they hated leaving the site when they had just begun to investigate. They found their way back to the main entrance to Mount Zohngnan. It turned out to be a good way away from the other more visited spots on the mountain. Though it had found honor on the fundamentalist Taoist mountain centuries ago, it did not enjoy a prominent position. Until recent years when it was discovered that the temple was an early Christian church, there was no maintained path that led to it. It was considered a safety hazard because of its precarious lean.

It was not hard to find a taxi. The visiting hours to the mountain were almost over, and there was a line of taxies waiting to meet the many stragglers coming out needing rides. Jamisen used a hotel brochure to show the driver where they wanted to go. Clip was impressed with his foresight in many of the matters that had come their way on the trip.

The driver dropped them off in front of the hotel. All three were famished, so they ate quickly in a back room of the hotel restaurant before going to their room. Each one slept soundly with their personal dreams of how the scroll would be found.

The next morning they woke early and had a quick bite of toast, hard boiled eggs, and rice in the same back room of the hotel restaurant. They left the hotel in search of the supplies they would need while searching the temple area. They found a large store that had a plethora of merchandise for sale, everything from clothes to can-openers.

Mr. Estes bought Jamisen and himself a flashlight and extra batteries. Clip felt one step ahead for a change since he had already packed one. He also bought a small hand-held lantern, a Phillip's head screwdriver, and a flathead screwdriver. Then he bought Jamisen and Clip each a pocketknife. "You will have to get rid of them before we board a plane, but they might come in handy between now and then."

They picked out some food that would do for a couple meals. It was mostly dried meat of some kind that came in sealed plastic bags, dried rice cakes, several candy bars, and some bottled water. They stuffed all this in their backpacks with no room to spare.

They ate lunch at a café that specialized in dumplings with meat and vegetables inside. They took their time, for they did not want leave right away and have to spend too much time on the mountain for fear of becoming conspicuous. They sipped hot tea after the meal and discussed where the scroll might be hidden in or around the temple.

"I didn't see any fish," said Clip.

"Fish? Oh, you mean from the directions, *Tread 300 in the way of the fish,*" replied Jamisen.

"Yeah. Do you think the fish are inside the temple? Maybe the steps have fish on them or something like that."

"It is possible," said Mr. Estes. "You know, the only correlation that Lohn and I could make with fish is that is has long been one of the symbols of Christianity. Many of the apostles were fishermen. Jesus said he would make them *fishers of men.* Also, when Christians were persecuted by Rome, the fish was used as a signal to identify one believer to another. For instance, if two men met at a crossroads and one was a Christian, he might take his staff or his toe and draw a quarter circle in the dirt nonchalantly. If the other stranger was a Christian, he would draw a quarter circle connected to the other one at the front and crossing at the back to form the shape of a fish. This way Christians could identify each other without exposing themselves."

"I hope the fish we are looking for is not on the ground, or it will be impossible to find after all these centuries," said Clip thinking about the area they had seen around the temple the day before.

"*If* it is even still there," Jamisen said echoing Clip's doubts.

"We shall see, boys. I think there might be something inside the temple that will help us. At any rate, we didn't have time to do a thorough examination of the temple area yesterday. Tonight we will have plenty of time to search the inside and tomorrow, the outside, if all goes well."

Chapter 10

As it turned out, all *did* go well that evening. They took another taxi to Mount Zohngnan. Mr. Estes bought their admission passes to the mountain, while Jamisen and Clip bought some food from a vendor to eat later in the evening. They made their way along the twisting and turning path that led to the pagoda. As the day before, they did not see or hear anyone in the vicinity they were traveling. They reached the pagoda a couple of hours before dark and made some cursory scans of the area around the pagoda, but soon Mr. Estes suggested they enter it while they could still benefit from the sunlight.

Mr. Estes took off his backpack and unzipped one of the pockets. He produced the screwdrivers that he had purchased that morning. "Here you go, Clip. See if you can use this as a key to get us in."

Clip took the screwdrivers and studied the bracket on the door to which the lock was clasped. He used the Phillip's screwdriver to remove the screws, and then he used the flathead to pry the bracket from the door where it was stuck after years of attachment.

The heavy door swung open freely with a loud creak and whine. "Well, Clip. We will make a burglar of you yet."

They each got out their flashlights from their packs and very cautiously crept in through the entrance. The floor, eaves, and walls were covered with dust. There were footprints on the floor, presumably from the workmen who were repairing the temple. The open area of the first floor was much smaller than it looked from the outside because the walls were so thick. From the space left open for the door, the walls looked about fifteen feet in thickness. Mr. Estes explained this was for support purposes.

They did a thorough search of the first floor and found no markings or signs whatsoever. They took an old, partially rotten stairway up to the second floor. The open, usable area on this floor was much larger. There were two, large window openings on opposite sides of the level in which the failing light of the day shone through. They spent a half hour searching this level for any clues, but all they found was some ancient Chinese graffiti.

They had no more luck on the third floor, and by the time they reached the fourth floor, the sun had gone down completely, and they had to use the lantern and flashlights to see anything. Nothing was found on this floor either. The flooring on the fifth floor was more broken and rotten than the other floors, so they had to exercise great caution. Most of the floor was too far gone to even walk on, and they had to scan half the level from a distance.

The sixth and seventh floor yielded no better results. The allure and mystery of finding the scrolls had been intoxicating for the boys since they had first learned about them. Now that they were at the point of actually trying to get one, it seemed more difficult than it had in Mr. Estes' room at Stansberry. After applying what they knew, there was no 'X marks the spot' to be found.

Mr. Estes suggested they take a break and eat supper, so they made a picnic on the seventh floor. They ate in silence for a while. All three were well off the 'adrenaline high' they had been on when they had entered the pagoda. Clip finally asked the question that was at the forefront of all their minds. "What now?"

Mr. Estes looked contemplative. "Well, we don't know what we are looking for really. We have seen no fish or anything like a fish. To be honest, I thought you were on to something when you mentioned that the steps in the temple might have something to do with the *treading* part. I figured there might be

300 steps with fish on them or something that led to the top of the temple where the scroll would be hidden in the floor or wall. I suppose that would have been too easy. I always imagined the hard part was spending all those years figuring out the directions, but I see now—that may not be true.

"My biggest fear is that Lohn and I got the directions wrong somehow. At the time, the line seemed to be the only logical sequence of words, but we may have missed something. I think now all we can do is pray and ask for the Lord's help and guidance. It may be that we will have to regroup and sift through the code again and see if there is a different wording that will make sense."

This seemed like an awful alternative to Jamisen and Clip. "Will we have to go back to Stansberry?" Jamisen asked tentatively.

"No. I suppose we could go back to the hotel and call Lohn. I have all the dissemination of the code on my laptop, along with the Scripture that is supposed to correlate to it, so we could work on it here."

With that, Mr. Estes rose from where he was sitting and knelt on one knee. "Dear Lord, we are stumped. I guess we expected to walk right in and find the scroll waiting on us. It has been through Your grace and mercy that we were able to make it this far. Please guide us now and open our minds to possibilities we may have overlooked. In Your son Jesus' name I pray, amen."

Jamisen and Clip felt moved and a little invigorated by the prayer. They renewed their search with newfound enthusiasm. Once more they scanned the temple one level at a time. This time they took extreme care to search out every nook and cranny. Every crack and ledge was scrutinized for a movable stone or board.

After several hours of intense searching, they found themselves at the seventh level again, having worked their way down and back up again. Their spirits were heavy as lead. "Well, boys. I guess it's back to the drawing board tomorrow. Don't let this little setback get you down. The scrolls were not meant to be found easily. We will take a look at the Scriptures the code makes reference to, and maybe you two will catch a word or two that will make more sense than *Tread 300 in the way of the fish."*

It was deep in the night. They were all tired, and their eyes hurt from squinting in the dim light of the flashlights and the lantern. They made themselves as comfortable as possible on the seventh level. Using their extra clothes and backpacks, they made make-shift pallets on which they could sleep. Jamisen made his bed by one of the large windows and stared out at the stars and crescent moon.

He fell asleep staring out the window. His sleep was fitful, as was Clip's and Mr. Estes.' It was difficult to get comfortable on the hard floor, and every time they woke, their thoughts were bent to where the scroll might be found.

Jamisen was awake when the first light of morning began to appear through the window. The sun had not risen over the mountaintops, but faint illumination spread over Mount Zohngnan. He was staring out the window in almost the same position he had fallen asleep earlier that night. He watched the stars disappear one by one as the new day began. All of a sudden he jumped up and examined the right vertical side of the window. He ran his hand across the stone surface that had been quarried and smoothed centuries ago. He brushed the layers of dust away and traced a figure that was faintly chiseled in the stone.

"Wake up! Wake up! I've found it!"

Mr. Estes and Clip both sat up blearing eyed and startled. "What? What have you found?" Clip said rubbing his eyes and stretching as he walked toward the window.

"I think I've found the fish!"

Mr. Estes and Clip were both wide-awake now. They crowded in beside Jamisen to study the window. "See, right here." He traced the two curving lines that touched at one end and crossed at the other to make the body of a fish.

"I saw it when the light hit it. You wouldn't notice it just looking out the window. You have to be looking at an angle."

Mr. Estes traced the line with his fingers. "I think you are right. Now we need to figure out what it means."

"Could it be hidden behind the stone?" Clip asked.

Mr. Estes felt the edges of the stone that was about a cubic-foot in size. "I don't think so. It is sealed tightly to the other stone with mortar."

"What if the stone behind it had a hollowed out place for the scroll?" Jamisen suggested.

"Hmm. You might be right. Clip, see if you can find something among the tools outside to remove the stone. We will have to hurry, though. It won't be long before people will be coming to the mountain."

Clip hurried down to the outside of the temple and began looking for something to remove the stone. He returned in about fifteen minutes with a small sledgehammer that was covered in dried mud from being left outside. He had also brought the short, metal rod that he was going to use two days before to pry off the lock.

Jamisen held the rod tip against the mortar line while Clip hit it with the hammer. The job was easier than they thought it would be, for the ancient mortar crumbled easily away in small pieces with each stroke of the hammer. The only bad part was that each fall of the hammer sounded like a gunshot to them as it echoed in the temple. All they could do was hope that the sound didn't carry far enough for anyone around to hear it and pay it heed. After an hour of careful chiseling, the stone was free of the mortar enough that it could be pried out. Mr. Estes used the bar to free it, while Jamisen and Clip lowered it to the ground.

They were disappointed though. There was nothing behind the stone, other than another stone. "Dang it!" Clip said in exasperation. "That was a big waste of time."

"Now what?" Jamisen asked.

Mr. Estes paced the room in a small circle with his hands in his pockets. His head was down, staring at the floor in concentration. "I think we were too hasty and did not fully think about the directions. They say: *Tread 300 in the way of the fish.* Tread means walk, so maybe we are to walk somewhere, and the fish is a guide."

"Where are we going to walk to–out the window?" Clip asked staring at the ground seven stories below.

"Maybe we are to walk from the bottom of the temple and in the direction the fish is pointing. We could take 300 steps and see what we come across," Mr. Estes answered.

"It's worth a try," said Jamisen. "Why don't Clip and I go down and try it, and you can stay up here and guide us in the right direction. The fish was pointing that way," he said pointing into the forest that led to a group of small mountains about two miles away.

"Very well. That sounds like a good idea. I don't suppose we should replace the stone. It might fall out with no mortar to hold it and injure someone. Take your things, for we might not be returning."

Jamisen and Clip gathered all their belongings and hoisted their packs. They made their way down the stairs with renewed vigor. Once they were outside, they aligned themselves with the window, with their backs to the temple. They decided to walk about ten yards apart, with Clip on the left and Jamisen on the right, in case either was off course. This way they would have a better chance of not missing anything, though they still did not know for what they were looking.

They counted out loud as they took normal strides away from the temple. After about fifty strides, Mr. Estes whistled from the window. They were wondering too far to the right, so he had them adjust their course a little to the left.

After 100 strides, they had entered the forest, and they could only see Mr. Estes in the window every so often between the tops of the trees. On stride 300, they stopped and looked around. Only the top most part of the temple could be seen from here, but it was so far away that they would not be able to make out any signs Mr. Estes gave them anyway. The area was dense with trees and undergrowth, but there were no structures or makers to be found. They took off their backpacks and placed them on the ground to mark where they had stopped. They began searching in an ever-widening circle from that spot. They still had no clue what to look for. "These trees were definitely not here when the scroll was brought here, so whatever we are looking for will have to be stone," Clip said as he studied the surrounding woods.

They had been searching for about ten minutes, and they were just about to go back and see if they needed to realign themselves and try again when Clip found a marking. He yelled for Jamisen to join him. Clip was kneeling by a rock about two feet tall and three feet wide. It was surrounded by shrubs and covered in lichen. "Right here, look."

On the side of the rock, near the ground, the 'X' shape of a fish tail could be seen. Clip scraped some lichen off to reveal the rest of the body. "You found it!" Jamisen said with excitement. "I'll run back and get Mr. Estes." With that he took off at a sprint.

Clip retrieved their backpacks. The rock was around fifteen yards to the left of where Clip had stopped after 300 strides. He cleaned the rest of the lichen off and beat back the shrubs surrounding the rock, so it would be easier to examine. He tried pushing on the rock, but it would not budge.

Mr. Estes and Jamisen came panting through the trees. They joined Clip in examining the rock. "Let's see if you can help me move it, Jamisen. I couldn't move it by myself a minute ago. There might be something under it." Jamisen and Clip tried pushing on the rock together, but it still would not budge.

Clip dug around the edges with his heel. "I think it is just the top of a big rock that is buried."

Mr. Estes looked in the direction the fish's head was pointing. "I think maybe we should try walking 300 paces again in the direction the fish is pointing. We can walk three abreast this time to have a better chance of finding something."

With their backs to the stone, they walked in the direction the fish was pointing, Clip at the left, Mr. Estes in the middle, and Jamisen on the right. They counted audibly and made as straight a line as possible away from the rock. Several times one of their courses would become obstructed by a tree or rock formation, and they would have to wait for that person to try and reorient themselves. Their strides took them deeper into the forest and closer to the mountains. They stopped at 300, and Jamisen was almost on top of a rock wider than the one that they had previously found but only half the height. It was covered in lichen as well. Jamisen kicked away the foliage and lay on his stomach to study the sides of the rock. Almost immediately he saw the faint outline of a fish carved in the side. "I've found it!"

Mr. Estes and Clip hurried over to the rock. Jamisen was scrapping off the lichen. "See. It's there, clear as crystal."

Mr. Estes studied the rock. "I think this rock was placed here. See if you boys can move it."

Jamisen and Clip dug out the bottom edge for a handhold, and together they were able to turn the rock over. They took a stick and dug in the wormy dirt where the rock had been, but they found nothing after a foot of excavation. "Should we keep digging?" Jamisen asked.

"No. I don't think so. I think maybe we should look for another marker again."

It was then they realized their mistake. They had rolled the rock over without first checking the exact way the fish was pointing.

"I think it was that way," Jamisen offered pointing ahead.

"Well, we will just have to try it," Mr. Estes said.

They shouldered their packs again and Clip grabbed Mr.

Estes' briefcase. They counted off their strides once again and stopped once more at 300, but this time none of them were at any marking. They sat down their packs where they stopped and began searching for any large rocks that might contain the sign. Once again, Jamisen found the rock, but it was far to the right of where they had stopped. The rock was barely visible among some laurel bushes, but the light color of the stone had stood out within the dark green foliage.

This stone also looked as if it had been placed there. It was more oval in shape than the previous one. The picture of the fish was very distinct on the base of one side. It was chiseled deeper than the other two had been. "Jamisen seems to have a knack for finding these things," Mr. Estes said. "You wait here, Jamisen, and Clip and I will get our stuff."

They returned with the packs and briefcase. The sun was high overhead now, and the rumblings of hunger were overcoming the adrenaline of the search. "Why don't we eat a bite before we look for the next marker?" Mr. Estes suggested.

That sounded good to the boys, and they made a brunch of some of the food they had packed. They were down to one bottle of water each, so Mr. Estes advised using it sparingly.

They felt at ease lounging by the rock. A cool breeze made the stifling heat of summer comfortable in the shade of the forest. The three companions talked of the good turn of events that had been an answer to prayer, and they talked of where the scroll might ultimately be hidden. Their excitement was high, but they felt very contented and unrushed now that they had discovered the meaning of the final line in the directions.

Mr. Estes finally voiced a concern that had not yet entered the boys' mind yet. "We need to make a decision. If we eat sparingly, we have enough food for two more meals. Do we go back for more provisions with a better idea about what we are doing, or do we forge ahead?"

Jamisen and Clip both agreed they wanted to keep moving ahead. Mr. Estes seemed to approve of this, so they finished their small meal and began their search for the next marker.

The next marker turned out to be quite easy to find. It was Mr. Estes this time that was standing not more than ten feet from the marker, a heavy rectangular stone about four feet long and a foot high. This pattern continued well into the evening with only minor setbacks. Twice they steered off course while taking their 300 strides, but after starting again at the marker, they were able to find the next one. So far they had found four more markers since their meal, for a total of eight. The sun was setting, so Mr. Estes suggested they make a camp by the marker stone they had just found. It was in a dense part of the forest, and the trees were so big and grew so close together that they almost formed a roof above them.

This was the point Clip felt most useful on the whole trip thus far. Having lived in the mountains all his life, he was at home in the outdoors. He and his friends had spent many weekends camping in the Smoky Mountains that surrounded their town. He went about fixing a lean-to shelter and fire pit. Mr. Estes had concurred with him that they were well away from civilization and could chance a fire. They had gradually been ascending up the foothills of the mountains they had seen from the temple. It was cooler here in the elevated forest, so a fire would provide what little warmth and light they would need.

Jamisen walked back to a stream they had crossed about a hundred yards back with the admonition from Mr. Estes to refill their water bottles but not to drink any of the water yet. Mr. Estes rested on the last marker stone they had found that day. Clip was making his fire pit near enough to the stone that it could be used as an easy place to rest. For the first time since Clip had known him, Mr. Estes looked old and run down. He did not even offer to help Clip as he worked to set up the little camp. Clip made a mental note of this and planned on mentioning it to Jamisen when he had the opportunity.

Jamisen returned with the water bottles filled to the top

and sat them on beside his pack. He went to gather firewood at Clip's request. It was almost completely dark now and Clip needed the light of the fire to help him finish the lean-to he had started building. Clip had cleared off a four-foot by four-foot section of ground of all leaves and small plants for his fire pit. He then took a stick and loosened up the dirt in the area. He took his foot and raked the loose dirt to the sides making a small circular mound encircling the area he cleared. He repeated this process two more times until he had about an eight inch deep pit. He then gathered softball size stones and placed them around the edges of the pit.

Jamisen returned with an armload of large sticks. He dropped them noisily by the hole Clip had just made. "Did you not get anything smaller for starter wood?" Clip asked eyeing Jamisen's haul.

"Starter wood? You said nothing about starter wood. You just said to go get firewood. So I went and got some wood."

Clip laughed. "I take it you never built a fire while at the abbey?"

"Of course I never built a fire at the abbey. The closest I've ever come to camping was last night at the temple."

"Well, you've got to have small sticks to get the fire going, then you put on the big stuff."

"*Small sticks*. Got it." With that he headed back to the perimeter of the camp to find what Clip had instructed.

He returned with an armload of small sticks and twigs. Clip took these and placed them teepee style around some dried leaves he had placed in the bottom of the pit. He took out a box of matches he had taken from the hotel in Beijing and lit the leaves in several places. The fire consumed the crispy leaves greedily, and soon the twigs Clip had placed around them caught fire as well. Clip added larger sticks every few minutes, until eventually he was adding some of the bigger stuff Jamisen had brought the first time.

The fire gave off a good light as it reflected off the trunks of the enclosure of trees that surrounded the camp. Clip finished the lean-to by the light of the fire. Clip had jabbed two sturdy sticks in the ground about eight feet apart. The sticks had Y heads on top, and he had placed a cross pole in the neck of each stick. About six feet from the cross pole, he drove into the ground several sticks and leaned them against the cross pole. He then covered these poles with green, leafy hemlock branches and large ferns. It was a basic half shelter that would do little more than keep the dew or light rain off of you, but it made the camp look more hospitable.

Mr. Estes began to revive a little by the glow of the fire. He asked Jamisen to bring the water bottles to him. He rummaged through his pack and produced a small pill bottle. "I thought we might need these somewhere along the line, although I didn't figure it would be out camping in the woods."

"What is it?" asked Jamisen as he handed him the water bottles.

"It's iodine pills. You put them in the water and it purifies it. I wouldn't trust any of the water in this country. These work great to kill anything that might be harmful, but it does add a bitter taste to the water."

He plopped one pill in each of the bottles, and handed them back to Jamisen. Having done all they could with the camp they settled down and broke out some of their provisions. They ate a small meal, wanting to save the better portion of their food for breakfast so they would have plenty of energy to start the day. Jamisen and Clip reclined against a log they had rolled by the fire, while Mr. Estes sat on the marker with his elbows on his knees. They talked of the day's events and what the next day might hold. Then, as night drew on, talk turned from the scroll to stories from their lives.

Mr. Estes told stories of his travels, most of which Clip had heard but enjoyed none the less. He told of his youth and his struggles to start his fledgling boat company. He told of his salvation and the sense of worth he felt in the service of God's

Kingdom. He told the boys it took a lifetime to build a witness but only a second to lose it. And he admonished them to keep this in mind as they lived their lives.

He also told them of a powerful lesson he had learned from a pastor he had known soon after becoming a Christian. "His name was Israel Torres. He preached a revival at my church only a few months after I was saved. I was in my twenties and still unsure as to what I wanted to do with my life. I happened to be at a diner he was eating at one morning, and he remembered me from the service. He invited me to sit and eat with him. We talked about trivial things, but soon he could tell there were deeper issues I was dealing with in my life. He told me something I will never forget, and I hope you boys won't either. He said: 'God won't take you anywhere His grace can't keep you, Ralph.' That was a turning point in my life. I let go of my inhibitions and started trusting in the Lord to lead and guide me. He has never failed me, boys; even when I have failed Him over and over."

Jamisen talked about his childhood and growing up in the orphanage. He related his salvation experience and what it meant to him to live and work in the abbey. He talked about how many of his childhood friends could not understand his decision and how some even ridiculed him.

Clip opened up about his desire to see the world and how lucky he felt to be a part of this expedition. He talked about his indecisiveness in picking a major to study in college and the pressure he felt to succeed for his parents. He also talked about his salvation experience and the lapses and regaining of faith he had had during his life.

Mr. Estes inwardly smiled at the way the boys talked as if they were old men reminiscing. He knew they did not realize they had lived but a fraction of their lives, and many more struggles and victories lay ahead of them.

The night sounds made the whole experience seem surreal to the three companions. To be camping in a forest in China and in search of the scroll was almost beyond their comprehension. Clip looked up through the boughs of the trees at the stars twinkling on the clear night. He felt a little lightheaded when he contemplated the situation in which he was a part.

They stared at the dying embers of the fire, not saying anything. Each was lost in his thoughts about what had been said and what might come. After a while, all three began to feel the weight of the day, and their eyes drooped and longed for sleep. Clip stoked the fire with most of the remaining wood and they made their way into the lean-to, less than ten feet from the fire. Ferns were plentiful in the forest, and Clip had used them not only on the roof but also to make a somewhat soft bed on which they could sleep.

They put Mr. Estes' briefcase under the shelter with them and covered it with two of the backpacks to keep any moisture off of it. All three fell almost instantly to sleep. The lean-to was roomy enough for them to lie comfortably within its limited protection, although Jamisen and Clip's feet stuck out the end.

They rested surprisingly well in the outdoor setting. The spirit of the search had put them in an adventurous mindset. Clip dreamed of finding the scroll and winning renown across the world. He dreamed of returning to Kawana a hero under the proud gaze of his parents. These dreams comforted him, but when he awoke in the morning, he felt silly having basked in the glory of his dreams. He knew no one would probably ever find out about his role in finding the scrolls. He knew no one would ever find out about the scrolls if they were found, especially not people in his small town.

They made no fire that morning. As a matter of fact, Clip took great pains to fill in the fire pit and cover it back over with leaves and sticks to hide any trace of it. They took down the lean-to and scattered the poles and limbs. They did not expect to see anybody in this wilderness, but they did not want to take a chance of getting in trouble if they did.

They ate the rest of their provisions for breakfast. Jamisen refilled their water bottles after the meal, and Mr. Estes added more iodine pills to purify it. The morning broke cloudy, but the threat of rain did not seem great. They hoisted their packs, and Jamisen took the first turn at carrying the briefcase. After orienting themselves with the marker, they headed toward the mountains again, audibly counting their strides.

They found the next marker without any trouble, but they encountered a problem with its position. During the centuries since it had been placed there, a tree had grown right beside it. As the trunk expanded, it had actually upturned the rock so that it was resting sideways against the base of the tree. Though the symbol was clearly visible on the stone, they had no way of knowing which way it had originally pointed.

With no clear idea of where the next one might lie, they continued on the line they had been walking. This did not lead them to a marker, so they had to backtrack and painstakingly begin again. They moved a little more to the left, but their search turned up nothing. They backtracked again and moved even more to the left, but once again their search turned up nothing. They returned to the marker for the third time, and frustration began to mount. This time they tried going to the far right of their first try, and still they had no success.

Jamisen offered a solution. "Why don't we walk in an arc toward the left most point we walked to earlier? If we can keep a rounded angle, we should stay 300 strides from the marker. Surely we can come across it."

Not wanting to backtrack and start again, Mr. Estes and Clip agreed readily to this idea. They fanned out about ten yards apart and made for the far left point from which they had walked earlier. They had not gone far when Mr. Estes found an oval stone that looked like a giant football. It was almost completely covered in lichen and a trailing vine that had choked out much of the undergrowth in that spot.

Clip used a stick to clean the rock off, and sure enough, they found a fish chiseled into one side of it. The fish pointed directly toward the mountains, and it was obvious to them that this would be where the markers would take them. They took their 300 strides in the direction the fish had pointed, and Clip found the stone easily under a large hemlock tree.

This was the eleventh marker thus far, and they were very close to where the mountains began to climb steeper. From their position within the dense forest, they could see granite slopes and rocky outcroppings on the side of some of the mountains that were in contrast to the green foliage of scrubby trees and bushes that covered the mountainside.

They decided to take a break and rest for a while. They had spent quiet a lot of time on the marker that had been uprooted by the tree, and it was well past noontime now. They drank some of their water, but only sparingly because they had seen no other streams. Mr. Estes provided a surprise when he produced three candy bars for them to eat.

"Enjoy it boys because that is definitely the last of the food."

They savored the chocolate and caramel, but the candy bars only slightly abated their hunger. They studied the mountains before them and wondered what was on the other side and if it would be necessary for them to find out. They had no more food, so if something did not give soon, they might have to return for more provisions. This idea did not appeal to any of them.

Mr. Estes suggested they push on while they still had daylight, so they positioned themselves with the marker and made for the mountains. It was not long before the number of trees became less and the foliage less dense. After 200 strides, they could see the base of one of the mountains and where it started to climb steeply.

Their 300th stride brought them to a rock face about fifteen yards wide at the base of the mountain. It was covered in lichen and vines of the same kind they had encountered earlier. Trees grew in front of it, but there was no stone with the mark to be found.

"Do you think it might be on the rock wall?" Clip asked.

"I bet it is," Jamisen said, and he started pulling the vines off the rock face.

It was difficult to work at cleaning off the rock face because the trees grew close to it, and the vines were a tangled mess. Jamisen and Clip jerked and pulled the vines with their hands and drug the debris away so they could get close to the rock wall and inspect it. It was covered in brown dirt where years of sediment sliding down when it rained had been trapped in the vines. Jamisen and Clip then used sticks to scrape the dirt and lichen off the rocks. It was tiring work on an empty stomach, but the sun was hidden behind the clouds, which made it somewhat cooler.

As they were scraping the rock face, Jamisen's stick scratched across an indentation that interrupted the side-to-side arch in which he was moving the stick. He ran the stick back over the same area and found there were grooves etched in the stone. After a few more swipes, he cleaned away a deeply chiseled picture of a fish about eight inches long and five inches wide. It was chiseled at least two inches into the rock face.

Jamisen gave a whoop of joy. "I've found it!"

Clip untangled himself from the hemlock tree he was working behind and came to inspect with Mr. Estes, who had been resting on a log nearby.

"Wonderful work, Jamisen," Mr. Estes said clapping him on the back.

"It's pointing straight up the rock face," observed Clip.

"I guess that means we go up," answered Jamisen.

The fish did indeed point up along the rock face. A ledge was about thirty feet above them, and then the mountain rose steeply past that. How big the ledge was or what was there they could not tell.

"Shall we take a look?" Clip asked Jamisen as they stared up at the ledge.

"I definitely can't climb the sides of mountains any more, especially ones this steep. You boys go and take a look and see if there are any directional clues up there."

"Which way should we go up?" asked Jamisen eyeing the rock face in front of him doubtfully. Heights were not big on his list of fun things to experience.

"Well, I guess straight up. There are handholds all the way up to that ledge it looks like. We can at least go up that far and see if there is anything to see."

"What if we find some way to go around the side?"

"That could take a long time. What's the matter? Afraid of a little climbing?" Clip said with a grin. He probably would not have been so light hearted about the situation if he had known the internal trauma Jamisen was experiencing.

"No. I'm not afraid. Let's go."

"Be careful, boys, and take your time."

Clip started up first. Once again, his growing up in the outdoors paid off. He scampered from one handhold to the next like a monkey. He crisscrossed the rock face several times until he finally made it to the ledge in only a few minutes. He turned to eye Jamisen, who was not making good progress. Clip coached him a little on which way to turn here and what to grab onto there, until Jamisen finally rolled onto the ledge gasping for breath. This was attributed more to nerves than physical exertion.

When Jamisen had collected himself, they took a look at the area that made up the ledge. It was about twenty feet long and fifteen feet wide. The ground was covered with rough grass, small juniper bushes, and loose rock and dirt that had accumulated where it had washed down the mountain. At the back, opposite the edge they had just climbed over, the rock face continued steeply up the mountain. It was covered with more vines and lichen. After tearing some of the vines away, they found it was not a smooth surface. There were cracks and sharp fissures hidden by the vines.

Clip yelled down to Mr. Estes what they had found so far, then he and Jamisen began cleaning off the rock face to see if there was another direction marker. They had not cleaned off very much when Clip discovered a large, flat stone that was leaning against the rock face at the far right of the ledge. It was about three feet high and three feet wide. It was jagged and irregular in shape, and it blended in well with the stone wall it was leaned against. Clip might have even overlooked it, if some of the vines hadn't found their way behind it. When he was pulling them off, these stuck and would not come lose. After inspecting them, Clip saw that they ran behind the rock.

He cleaned the rest of the vines and lichen off and gave a gasp of surprise. "Jamisen . . . look."

Jamisen hurried over to where Clip was bent over the rock. Chiseled on the rock was a circle of seven fish about six inches long. Their heads were all facing the center with their tails extended out. It almost looked like a picture of the sun with rays coming from it.

Jamisen and Clip exchanged excited glances.

"This could be it!" Clip said in excitement.

"Let's move it and see."

Jamisen grasped the top edge and tried to roll the rock to the side, but he could not budge it. "You'll have to help me."

Clip got on the opposite side and pushed while Jamisen pulled. Ever so slowly the rock gave way and rolled a quarter turn to the side. This exposed a hole a little smaller than the rock itself. They peered in, but the daylight only penetrated a few feet within.

"We need our flashlights," said Clip.

Jamisen brows furrowed at the prospect of climbing back down the rock face only to turn around and come back up again.

"I'll go get them," offered Clip. "You clear away the rest of these vines from the hole." Clip added this last part in hopes of making Jamisen feel like he was still contributing.

Clip nimbly made his way down the rock face. He explained what they had found to Mr. Estes, who flashed a grin from ear to ear. "We must be close now, Clip. I wish I could be up there to discover it with you, but this old body would never make it. You boys take your time, and I will hold down the fort here. Do you think I should start preparing another camp?"

Clip felt empowered by the fact Mr. Estes had asked his opinion in this decision. "No. I think if it is there, we will find it in plenty of time to make it back to the temple at least before dark. Even if we have to walk a little in the dark, it will be better than spending a hungry night out here."

Mr. Estes agreed. Clip put the two flashlights, the lantern, extra batteries, and he and Jamisen's water bottles in his backpack. He then climbed back up the rock face to where Jamisen was waiting.

Clip could see excitement on Jamisen's face that mirrored his own. He handed him his water bottle and they took some big gulps of water. "Well, are you ready to find a scroll?" Clip asked.

"I jolly well hope so, or we walked a long way 300 steps at a time for nothing."

Chapter 11

Clip handed Jamisen his flashlight, and he took out his own. They scanned the interior of the hole as far as their lights would go, but it was still too dim to make out anything definite. The hole was more like a tunnel that seemed to go down at an angle back into the mountain.

"Well, here we go," said Clip getting down on his hands and knees. He shined his light with his right hand and used his left hand to help him crawl awkwardly down the three-foot high tunnel. The floor of the tunnel was muddy where rainwater had seeped under the rock and was never exposed to the sun or wind. It did not take long for his hands and legs to become filthy and his pants to become soaking wet. His backpack kept scraping the top of the tunnel, and loose rock and dirt tumbled into his shirt.

After twenty feet, the height of the tunnel doubled in size, and Clip found he could stand up with no problem. Jamisen still had to stoop some though. The floor of the tunnel was level now and did not angle down. Clip froze in his tracks. "Do you hear that?"

Jamisen stopped quickly. Neither one breathed for a minute. "Yes. There is some kind of noise ahead."

Clip walked cautiously ahead. He shined his light in every nook and cranny at least twice before he took another step.

"Water."

"What did you say?" asked Jamisen in a whisper.

"Water. That's what we hear. There is water running somewhere up ahead."

After a few more yards, the distinct sound of a stream could be heard echoing through the tunnel. A few more yards and the tunnel opened up into a cavern about the size of a large hotel room. There was a small stream that issued from under the rock wall at the left side of the cavern. It trickled through a two-foot deep bed that had been cut out of the rock floor after thousands of years of wear. The twelve inch wide stream disappeared into a large crack on the other side of the cavern.

Clip opened his pack and removed the lantern. This enabled them to see almost the whole cavern without having to use their flashlights. The floor was muddy as the tunnel had been. The ceiling was about ten feet high with a few small stalactites hanging down from it. The walls were a shiny, mud color where moisture was on them. "I sort of expected to find the scroll locked up in a chest or something down here," Clip said as he scanned the floor and wall of the cavern.

They carried the lantern around exploring the room for any shelves or niches they might find. Instead, they found another tunnel on the other side of the stream. This one was about five feet high and about a foot wide.

"Blimey. That is a tight fit," Jamisen observed as he shined his light down the tunnel.

"Well, this has to be the way," said Clip taking off his backpack. "Let's put new batteries in our flashlights before we go down there."

"Torches, you uneducated 'Yank.'"

"What are you talking about?"

"They are called *torches*. I've let you and Mr. Estes get by with calling them *flashlights* until I'm about to burst. Do you not realize they produce no flash at all?" He laughed as he said this last part.

Clip chuckled. "Well, I'm afraid you are outnumbered on this expedition, so we'll keep calling them flashlights."

Clip put his flashlight in his pocket after adding new batteries to his and Jamisen's light. He held the lantern out in front of him and entered the tunnel. He had to turn his body sideways in order to enter. Jamisen was about to follow when he told Clip to wait. "Come back and take a look at this!"

Clip backed back out of the tunnel to see what Jamisen

had found. He was shining his flashlight above the tunnel entrance. "I saw it as I started to enter."

Clip held the lantern up to the spot Jamisen was inspecting. There were words carved into the stone. "It's Latin," said Clip.

"Yes, I know. Can you read it?"

"I can make out the words: hold, scroll, breath, and life. But I can't tell you what they mean in the phrase. I suppose a monk in training like you can read it."

"Without a doubt my good man. Listen and learn: *To hold the scroll, you must hold the breath of life.*"

"Is that it?"

"Yes."

"Are you sure?"

"Quite sure."

"Well, what does it mean?"

"I haven't the faintest idea."

Clip shined the lantern around the tunnel entrance and started examining the area all around it. "I don't know what the *'breath of life'* is, and I don't see anything that looks like it. What should we do?"

"I suppose we just go on and see what we find. We can always come back and see if we missed something."

"But what if there is a booby trap or something? You know, like off of an 'Indiana Jones' movie. What if we have to figure this out to keep from falling down a pit or getting stuck in the head by some spike that shoots out of the wall?"

"I think you are over dramatizing the situation. For one thing, that is the movies. This is real life. Secondly, don't you think that the priest who hid the scroll would have figured that if you got this far, you were probably meant to be the one who found the scroll?"

"What if someone found this place accidentally? What would keep some hiker from taking the scroll?"

"The Latin is the safeguard to whatever we have to figure

PETER'S PRAYER

out to get the scroll. How many people in China can read Latin? Let's just go down the tunnel, and the answer to the phrase might present itself."

"OK. You win, but I ought to make you go first since you don't believe in booby traps."

Clip entered the tunnel once more but slowly this time. He inspected every inch in front of him before he moved a step. Jamisen was poking fun at him from behind. "Watch out 'Indiana,' keep your whip ready."

"Laugh it up, funny boy. You know it's always the second guy who gets it after the first guy trips the booby trap."

Jamisen had a harder time of it than Clip because he had to crouch as he shuffled along sideways, and he was still constantly bumping his head. They had gone about ten-yards when the tunnel started to widen. They could walk straight now, without having to turn sideways.

Clip continued to step gingerly on the muddy floor. He expected any moment for the bottom to drop out or some other trap to get them. Suddenly, he was brought to a halt by what looked like a light shining ahead. "Do you see that?" he asked Jamisen in a whisper.

Jamisen peered over his shoulder. "I see a dim light ahead."

They moved slowly on, and the light started to move. Clip stopped again, and the light ahead stopped moving. He jiggled the lantern, and the light ahead moved again. "Ha, ha. It's reflecting off something up ahead."

Clip could hear Jamisen breathe an audible sigh of relief. They continued on several more yards, with the tunnel widening with each step. They were brought up short by a pool of water that filled the eight-foot wide tunnel from side-to-side. Jamisen shined his light across the pool and saw that it lapped against a stone wall on the far side. "It's a dead end," he said shining around the edges of the pool for another opening.

Clip took out his light and shined it down in the pool. It

was clear, and by the looks of it at least five or six-feet deep. The bottom was sandy, and there were tiny, pale minnows swimming around. "Well, this isn't a mud puddle. Water fills this pool from somewhere because there is fish in it. Do you see a box or anything down there that might have the scroll in it?"

Jamisen joined his light with Clip's, but neither one of them saw anything but the sandy bottom.

"What do we do now?" asked Clip.

"I don't know. We couldn't have missed another tunnel; unless there is something in the main cavern back there we missed."

"But what about the Latin writing above the tunnel entrance? That had to be a clue for something. Besides we searched all around that cavern."

"I suppose you are right. The inscription said: *To hold the scroll, you must hold the breath of life*. So what do we do with that?"

Clip kept repeating the words over and over out loud. "It must be symbolic of something, so what does the '*breath of life*' symbolize?"

Jamisen kept scanning the dead end with his light to try and find some clue. He then bent down on one knee and scanned the pool. He dipped his hand in the water. "Wheww. That's cold. A dip in that would take your breath away in a hurry."

"That's it! You're a genius," exclaimed Clip.

"What's it?"

"You said, 'take your breath away.' That's what the inscription meant. It wasn't symbolic. It was *literal*. *To hold the scroll, you must hold the breath of life*. You have to hold your breath to swim under water. You must have to go into the pool to get to the scroll."

"Blimey. We'll freeze to death!"

"That has to be the way, though. Look." Clip shined his light to the far end of the pool. "The water goes up under the rock wall over there. I bet we have to go under it."

"As bad as I hate to admit it, I believe you are right. How do we do it?"

"Well, we need one of the plastic bags we carried the food in to cover our lights. There are some empty ones in my pack. I'll go back and get it, since I fit through the tunnel better."

Clip hurried back to the cavern where he had left his backpack. He found two clear, plastic bags and made his way back to the pool. They wrapped their lights in the bags and took their shoes and socks off. "I suggest we strip down to our skivvies," said Jamisen. "That way we will have dry clothes to get into when we get out."

"Good idea."

They took off there clothes and immediately became chilled in the cool dampness. The prospect of jumping in the freezing water did not help to warm them either. Clip put his foot into the water. "Holy moly! It's freezing!"

"I told you."

"Well, there's nothing for it." Clip sat on his rear end and slid into the water, which came up to his shoulders. Immediately he convulsed from the shock of the cold. He held his light out of the water, and it was all he could do to hold onto it because he was shaking so badly.

Jamisen slid in next to him with similar results. "My dear Lord! I've . . . never . . . felt anything . . . so cold," he stammered between clenched teeth.

"Okay. Let's . . . get . . . this . . . over . . . with," Clip suggested. "I'll go . . . first . . . you . . . follow."

With that he took several deep breaths, trying to calm his body down, then he plunged under the water. Jamisen saw him swim down to the bottom of the rock wall, and in a few seconds his light disappeared. It then occurred to Jamisen that there might not be anywhere to go, and what if Clip tried to come back and Jamisen was blocking his way. He waited a few more seconds, but he did not see Clip's light again. He took several deep breaths as Clip had done and then plunged in after him. Jamisen's face and head felt like it was being stuck by thousands of tiny pins. He was concentrating on the pain so much that he was not doing a good job of swimming, so he tried to put it out of his mind and look ahead for Clip's light.

He was surprised how well he could see with his own light. He passed under the rock wall, which continued to be right above his head. There was only about a three-foot space separating the bottom of the pool and the rock above. Jamisen started feeling claustrophobic and panicky. He was starting to run out of breath, and there was still no sign of Clip. He was about to turn back when the bottom of the floor started slanting upward. He looked up and saw a light above and no rock. He pushed hard with his feet and swam toward the light. After about ten-feet, he came sputtering out of the water.

Clip was standing on a small ledge shaking all over with a huge smile on his face. With effort he made his blue lips work and said, "We've . . . found . . . it!"

Chapter 12

Jamisen forced his numb limbs to pull himself out of the water onto the ledge with Clip. They were in a large cavern, fully twice the size of the first one they found. It was completely full of water except for a ledge here and there—like the one on which they were standing. Clip shined his light on the wall behind them. "Look at this."

There was a niche carved into the wall about eighteen-inches high, six-inches wide, and ten-inches deep. In it rested a clay vessel about the size of a thermos. Above the niche was another Latin inscription chiseled into the stone. "What does that say?" Clip asked shining his light on it. The cold was forgotten for the moment, and their bodies were warming from the adrenaline rush.

"*God will hear and answer.*"

"This is it, Jamisen. We've really found it."

Clip handed Jamisen his light, and gingerly lifted the vessel. He half expected another task, some last trick of the cavern, but nothing happened. They inspected it carefully. The lid had a wax-like substance that sealed it.

Clip felt of the edges and sides. It was completely smooth. "We'd better not open it until we get out of the cave and Mr. Estes can see it. Besides, we need to keep it sealed to get back through the water."

"Let's get started while I can still move my body. I'm the coldest I've ever been in my life."

They put the vessel in Clip's plastic bag for extra protection, and Jamisen put both lights in his bag. "You take the lights, and I'll follow right on your heels so I can see the light," Clip said.

"OK. Let's do it." They lowered themselves back into

111

the cold water. It was not as much of a shock this time because their bodies were already numb.

"Ready?" Jamisen asked.

"Ready."

They took some deep breaths in unison, and then Jamisen plunged under the water. Clip followed with the vessel tucked tightly under his arm. The trip back was quicker and less anxious since they both knew the distance. They surfaced on the other side of the pool and climbed out in a frigid heap.

They dried themselves as best they could with a shirt Clip had left in the backpack and put on their clothes. This warmed them some, but both boys were trembling, and their teeth were chattering.

"We've got to . . . get . . . moving, . . . or we're going to get . . . hypothermia," Clip said shakily.

"OK. You . . . carry the scroll . . . and I'll carry . . . the lantern."

They made their way back through the skinny tunnel and to the first cavern. Jamisen only slowed down long enough to reach down and grab Clip's backpack, which he hoisted on his own back. They crawled back up and out the small, muddy tunnel into the fresh air. It was dusky outside. The tip of the sun was barely visible on the horizon. It felt warm to the boys, and some of the life started to return to their limbs.

"Should we roll the stone back?" asked Jamisen.

"I suppose it couldn't hurt."

Clip set the vessel down gently and helped Jamisen roll the stone back where they had found it. They even pulled down some overhanging vines to partially cover it up again. They did not know why, but it felt like they should keep the place hidden from future disturbances.

Jamisen looked over the edge for Mr. Estes. "I don't see him down there."

"He's probably sitting on a log nearby or even taking a

nap. I noticed last night he was starting to feel the wear and tear of tramping through the woods."

Jamisen gave Clip his backpack, and Clip put the vessel in it to free up both his hands for the descent. Both boys made it down with no problem. They looked around for signs of Mr. Estes, but he was nowhere to be found. They heard a rustling in the bushes to their left and then someone yelped.

"Run, boys! Run!"

Thump.

"Owww."

"I told you to keep your hand over his mouth!" said a man with a heavy Italian accent.

"He bit my hand!"

Clip whirled around toward the voices. He knew it was Mr. Estes, and he knew Mr. Estes was warning him, but he was frozen in place, as was Jamisen. Just then two men came out of the bushes. It was Danner and Rollins, the two men who had been with the bishop. Danner had Mr. Estes by the back of the throat with one hand and his arm in the other. The bishop appeared from behind them.

"Run, Clip! Now!" Mr. Estes yelled.

Clip's mind finally sprung into action. He hated to leave Mr. Estes, but he knew that he and Jamisen needed to get away and regroup if they were to help him. He grabbed Jamisen by the arm and spun around to run when Bell walked from behind a tree pointing a revolver at them.

"Easy, fellas. Don't take off just yet."

Clip and Jamisen stopped short. Clip's heart was pounding in his throat. He looked at Jamisen, who was pale as a ghost. The thought of dying on this trip had never entered Clip's mind, and the surreal situation was making his knees weak.

"Now, we don't want to hurt you boys, so just go and stand over there by Mr. Estes. We'll get this over with quickly, and you'll be eating egg rolls in Louguan before the night is over."

Danner had released Mr. Estes, and he was standing by the rock face messaging his swelling jaw. He had obviously paid a price for trying to warn the boys.

"How did you find us?" Jamisen asked.

"It was easy enough," Sorlenni answered. "When we were talking at the hotel, Mr. Danner pinned a small tracking device to one of your bags."

Danner walked over and picked up Jamisen's pack where he had left it on the ground before climbing the rock face. He held it up and gave a quick jerk on one of the adjustment buckles. In his hand, he held a tiny black disk the size of a button. It would have been indistinguishable from the pack unless a person was looking for it.

Sorlenni smiled. "It was simple enough to follow your signal. Although, I did not relish sleeping outside two nights in a row."

The bishop walked casually up to Clip with his hands clasped behind his back. "I think you have something we would all be very interested in seeing."

"It wasn't there," Clip answered with a snarl.

"Somehow I don't believe you. Take off your bag and open it."

Clip took a step back. "No."

"Either take it off or Mr. Danner and Mr. Rollins will take it off for you."

Mr. Estes stepped in front of Clip. "OK. This is gone far enough Sorlenni. You are a man of God; a high servant of the Church. Will you actually partake in harming someone? Let us go now, while you still have some dignity left."

"You are right, Ralph. I will not partake in harming anyone, but I can assure you Mr. Bell and his associates have no compunction about harming anyone. Now open the bag!"

As if to reinforce what Sorlenni had said, Bell stepped toward Clip and pointed the revolver at Clip's head and cocked it.

"OK. Wait!" cried Mr. Estes stepping between Clip and the gun. "Open the backpack, Clip."

Clip unshouldered the pack and set it on the ground. Bell uncocked the gun, but he still pointed it at Clip, who knelt down and unzipped the pack. He removed the vessel and held it up to Sorlenni. The bishop took it gently from his hands as if he were cradling a child.

A soft gasp escaped his lips as he held the vessel up to the dying light of day. He inspected the seal around the lid. "Mr. Rollins, your knife please."

Rollins produced a switchblade knife which he promptly flicked open. Sorlenni held the vessel with both hands, while Rollins cut away the seal. After a few minutes of careful slicing, the lid was completely free. Sorlenni took off the lid and handed it to Rollins. He then turned the vessel upside down, and out slid a small scroll with a wax seal.

This was the moment for which Clip had been waiting. All eyes were on Sorlenni and the scroll. When Clip had removed the vessel from his backpack, he had seen the Phillip's head screwdriver Mr. Estes had given to him to open the door to the temple. He was still kneeling by the backpack when Sorlenni opened the lid on the vessel, and he had slid his hand in the pack and quickly grabbed the screwdriver when all eyes were on the appearance of the scroll.

"At last!" said Sorlenni with a demented smile on his face.

Just then Bell let out a scream. All eyes turned to see Bell grasping at a screwdriver that was imbedded in his thigh up to the handle. In a flash, Clip had snatched the gun from Bell's hand in his moment of shock.

Bell cursed and made a grab at Clip who jumped back and aimed the gun at him. "You better give me back the gun while you are still able, kid!"

Clip jumped back another step. "Don't come any closer!"

he said in a trembling voice. The moment was almost too much for him. The adrenaline was blasting through his body.

"You won't shoot. We all know it. Give me back the gun, and we'll let you go. We've got what we want now." Bell took another step toward Clip.

With that step, something clicked in Clip. Like a badger backed in his hole, Clip's survival instinct kicked in, and he saw the situation clearly. Steady as a rock, he looked Bell square in the eye and said, "Try me," as he cocked the gun and pointed it at Bell's forehead, not two-feet away.

This brought Bell to a halt. "Now move over there and sit down," Clip said pointing beside Sorlenni.

Then, before Clip had time to react, the tables turned in a flash. Rollins reached out and grabbed Jamisen by the nape of his neck and pulled him toward him with his knife at Jamisen's throat. "Now, boy, you still want to play? Throw down the gun."

He held Jamisen in front of him like a shield. To show he was serious, Rollins pricked Jamisen's skin with the tip of the knife, and a tiny trickle of blood ran down his neck. Clip could see his jugular vein pulsing, as Rollins kept his head jerked back in a strain.

A moment of hesitation fueled by fear gripped Clip, but only a moment. He stepped to within six-feet of Rollins and turned the revolver to where it pointed it at his head. "You know, I never understood situations like this when they happened in the movies."

They all looked at Clip wondering where he was going with this, including Mr. Estes and Jamisen.

"It always seemed dumb to me to give in to the demands of a guy holding a gun or a knife to somebody. Because if you kill Jamisen, I'm going to shoot you. Sure he might be dead, but we'll all be dead if I throw down this gun. So, I'm going to count to three, and if you haven't turned him loose, I'm going to put a bullet in the bishop's head that a bird could fly through."

He turned and placed the gun against Sorlenni's temple. "Then whether you slit his throat or not, I'm going to do the same to you."

"He's bluffing," said Bell who was still sitting on the ground with the screwdriver sticking out of his thigh.

"ONE!"

Rollins looked at Bell and then at Sorlenni who was standing there with his eyes closed.

"TWO!" Clip cocked the hammer of the gun. At the sound of the retraction of the hammer, Sorlenni's eyes flew open.

"Th . . ."

"Release him!" Sorlenni said as he exhaled the breath he had been holding since Clip placed the gun on his temple.

Rollins hesitated and then pushed Jamisen away from him.

"Now drop the knife," Clip ordered.

Reluctantly, Rollins threw the knife down. "Now, all of you go and sit by Bell. Danner, Rollins, and Sorlenni shuffled over to where Bell was seething in anger. His pant's leg was now soaked with blood.

Mr. Estes and Jamisen walked over and stood beside Clip. Jamisen's eyes were as big as saucers as he held his hand to his throat to stop the small cut from bleeding.

"Hand Mr. Estes the scroll Sorlenni."

Sorlenni held up the scroll to Mr. Estes who took it and carefully placed it in a plastic bag Jamisen handed him from his backpack.

"You know we will find you again," said Sorlenni with malice in his eyes. "By taking the scroll, you are sentencing yourself to a life of hiding with it."

"Oh, we are not going to hide the scroll, Sorlenni," answered Mr. Estes. "We are going to *read* it."

The thought of reading the scroll had never occurred to the bishop who wanted to covet it and use it as a religious icon to loiter over peoples' heads. He looked confused and uncomprehending at what Mr. Estes had just said.

"I guess we should just kill you then, so that you won't follow us," Clip said.

"You don't have it in you kid," said Bell with a mock grin.

"You know, you are probably right, but I promise you I'm not above shooting a man in the leg, so I would not try and follow us today."

"I wish we had some rope to tie them up with," said Mr. Estes.

"I have a better idea," said Jamisen speaking for the first time.

He whispered his plan to Mr. Estes and Clip. Clip laughed out load. "That's perfect!"

"OK. On your feet," Clip said directing them with the gun. The four stood up, Bell with the aid of Danner. "Now, take off all your clothes."

"What? Are you mad?" said Sorlenni.

"Nope, but we don't have any other way to keep you from following us. Somehow I don't think we can trust you to stay here until we get away, so start undressing."

Danner, Rollins, and Bell complied. Bell had to remove the screwdriver, which elicited more cursing from him. The bishop stood there for a moment trying to comprehend how one moment he was holding the scroll and the next he was ordered to stand naked in the middle of a forest. When reality finally set in, he took off his clothes.

All four stood there in their underwear. Bell had dried blood all over his leg. Clip did allow him to rip his shirt and tie it around his thigh to help stop the bleeding.

"Everything," said Clip evenly.

"No. I refuse," said Sorlenni.

Bell, Rollins, and Danner, who were used to standing on the other side of the gun, understood the logic behind Clip's order as something they would do and complied again grudgingly.

"You can either do it, or I'll put a bullet in your leg to prevent you from following us," Clip said to Sorlenni.

The hatred Sorlenni had exhibited before was nothing compared to the boiling rage he felt toward Clip, now. Jamisen collected all their clothes and took Rollin's knife and cut strips out of their shirts and pants. He used this to tie their hands and arms. He, Clip, and Mr. Estes shouldered their own packs and carried the packs that belonged to Bell and the rest to discard when they were well away from there.

"Now," said Clip in a commanding tone. "We are leaving. If by some chance you get untied, I would suggest not following us. I can promise I'll aim for a leg if I see you again, but I can't promise I won't hit something else."

With that, Jamisen and Clip turned and started walking away. Mr. Estes walked over to where the bishop was sitting on the ground tied at the hands and feet. "What happened to you? When did you choose to stray from God?"

Sorlenni would not even look at him, so Mr. Estes followed behind Jamisen and Clip.

Chapter 13

They tried to walk as fast as they could through the woods, but it was almost completely dark now. They stumbled, tripped, and bumped their way along in the direction Clip best guessed the temple. After a half hour of nonstop walking, they stopped for a break. Clip took out the lantern to inspect what was in the backpacks they were carrying.

Jamisen punched Clip's shoulder in a friendly manner, *"Whether you slit his throat or not, I'm going to do the same to you? I'm glad he didn't try."*

Clip grinned. "What else was I supposed to do?"

"I don't know, but I hope you were bluffing."

"To be honest, I didn't know what I was going to do when I hit three," Clip said with a laugh of relief.

"I'm just thankful we didn't have to find out. You boys did a great job back there. To be honest, I thought we had lost the scroll and possibly our lives," said Mr. Estes, who was sitting on a log with his head bent low. He looked terrible. His breathing was quick and shallow.

"Are you all right, Mr. Estes?" Clip asked with concern.

"Yes." He said raising his head and forcing a smile. "I'm just a little tired."

Clip went back to inspecting the contents of the backpacks. He found several hundred dollars and several thousand Chinese Yuan, which he handed Jamisen. He also found all of their passports. There was a folder in one backpack that contained pictures of Mr. Estes, Jamisen, and Clip and a log of their movements since arriving in China.

"What do we do with their stuff?" asked Jamisen.

"Well, I know what I'm doing with these." He scraped

away a spot on the ground until he had exposed the dirt. He then took out the box of matches and set the passports on fire. It only took a couple of minutes for them to burn up completely. Clip stomped on the ashes and covered over the spot again.

Jamisen found a large, dead tree nearby that had broken near its base. He took the backpacks and stuffed them down in it, and then he covered them with leaves and sticks to hide them.

"I think we better get moving again, especially if we want to get back in time to get a taxi near the entrance to Mount Zohngnan. Mr. Estes rose with a slight groan. He looked pale and was still sweating profusely. Clip grew even more worried about his condition, but Mr. Estes refused his or Jamisen's aid.

The forest was dark as if a black velvet blanket was stretched across the treetops. They never would have made it at the limited speed they were going if they did not have the use of their lights. The going was still slow, partly because of the darkness and partly because Mr. Estes seemed to be waning with each step. They were forced to take another break less than an hour after their first one because of Mr. Estes' worsening condition.

The trees were thinning, so they knew they were coming to the edge of the forest, but they still were not completely sure if they were on line to come out near the temple. Mr. Estes made the boys push on, saying they could not afford to stop long on his account.

After another hour and two more rest breaks, they broke from the forest and entered a field. To their immediate left they could make out the silhouette of the temple several hundred yards away. They had come out south of where they had entered the forest two days before. Mr. Estes seemed to walk easier in the field, and his demeanor even seemed to improve to Clip.

They reached the temple with no problem, then made their way to the entrance gate of the mountain. It was about nine o'clock, and there were a few taxi's left for stragglers and employees who worked around the mountain.

When they fell into the taxi, it was like a great weight lifted off of Jamisen and Clip's shoulders. "Louguan," said Jamisen. The taxi driver nodded and sped down the road honking at everything that moved.

"We made it," Clip said with a tired smile.

"I'm famished," said Jamisen. "After we find another hotel we have to eat."

"Should we stay in Louguan, or go back to Xi'an?" Clip turned and asked Mr. Estes.

He looked pale again, and he was still sweating. He was breathing irregular, and flecks of spittle were in the corners of his mouth.

With some effort he said, "Xi'an, if we can find transportation."

When they arrived in Louguan, they had to find another taxi because their driver refused to go to Xi'an. They had the driver drop them off in front of the first hotel to which they came. "Maybe we should stay here tonight and let you rest, Mr. Estes," Clip said in a worried voice.

"No. We need to get as far away as possible. We must try and fly out of Xi'an tomorrow."

Jamisen took the money they had taken from the backpacks and went to hire another taxi. Clip stood by Mr. Estes lending him his shoulder for support and trying to decide what he could do to help him. It was not long before Jamisen motioned them to join him at one of the taxis. "He is willing to take us, but it took giving him some of the U.S. dollars."

"Great."

Mr. Estes flopped into the back seat, while Jamisen and Clip loaded their backpacks into the trunk. It was then that a terrifying realization hit him. "The briefcase!"

"What?"

"Mr. Estes' brief case. We left it back at the rock," Clip said with a look of anguish on his face. "I thought I was real smart, pulling all that off, and we walked right away and left them with the directions to the other two scrolls. It must have been in the bushes where they were hiding when we came down." Clip put his hand to his head and started messaging his temple, which was starting to pound.

"All that is on the laptop is the coded directions. As far as I remember, there are no specific locations given. It took years for Lohn and Mr. Estes to figure out the locations. Besides, the laptop has one of those fingerprint scanners that you have to use before you can access it. I saw Mr. Estes using it at the abbey and the hotel once."

"Yeah, but there were maps in the briefcase and on the laptop. I'm sure they are maps of the countries where the other two scrolls are. It wouldn't take a genius to use the directions to narrow a place down, especially if you know what country it is in. We're so stupid." Clip pounded the trunk of the car.

"What about the finger print scanner? They can't even get to the directions if they can't access the files."

"You know as well as I do that a halfway decent computer hacker will be able to get those files out. You are forgetting something else, too."

"What?"

"Our passports, and most of our money was in the briefcase."

"Do we tell Mr. Estes?"

"I don't think we should right now. He looks like he's had it. I don't think news like this would make him feel any better. We just need to pray they forget it's in the bushes."

They loaded into the car, with Jamisen sitting up front. The taxi driver made good time, for the traffic was light this time of night. The hunger pains they had been feeling had turned to a dull tightening in their stomachs, and all three of them dozed off to sleep from fatigue.

The honking of the many horns on the streets woke Jamisen. He rubbed his eyes and saw that they were at the outskirts of the city.

"Hotel," he said to the driver, who looked confused. "Hotel," Jamisen said again as put his hands over his head forming a pointed roof. He then clasped his hands together and closed his eyes in mock sleep.

The driver nodded his head in understanding. In a few minutes, he pulled up in front of a hotel on the west side of the city. Jamisen started counting out the Yuan to pay the driver. "Hey, wake up back there."

Clip stirred and yawned. "Are we there?"

"Yes. This looks like a decent enough hotel."

"As long as it has a bed and something to eat in there I don't care." Clip gently shook Mr. Estes' arm. "Mr. Estes, we are at the hotel."

He did not move. "Mr. Estes," Clip said again shaking his arm harder, but still he did not stir at all. "Jamisen, something is wrong with Mr. Estes!"

Jamisen was already out of the car. He stuck his head back in the door. "What's wrong?"

"He won't wake up!"

"Check his pulse!" Jamisen said rushing around to Mr. Estes' door.

Clip put his hand to Mr. Estes' neck. "I feel a pulse, but he's pale as a ghost. We've got to get him to a hospital!"

By this time the driver was out of the car staring at the scene and speaking Chinese a mile a minute. "Hospital! Hospital!" Jamisen said to the driver as he pointed to Mr. Estes.

It did not take the driver long to figure out Mr. Estes was sick. The driver jumped back in the car, and Jamisen ran back to the passenger side and climbed back in and slammed the door shut. The driver started talking on a CB radio that was mounted on his dash. Someone answered him through the static, and they had a brief conversation. He seemed to Jamisen and Clip he was getting directions. In a moment he replaced the CB and said, "OK. OK," as he nodded his head to Jamisen and Clip. He started the car and sped back into the flow of traffic.

Clip was an emotional wreck. He had never felt so helpless in his life. He could still feel a faint pulse on Mr. Estes, but he seemed to be barely breathing at all. The only thing he could think to do was pray, so he prayed the whole agonizing ride to the hospital. He did not know what Jamisen was doing, for he did not say a word. But he figured he was probably doing the same thing.

In less than ten minutes the driver stopped in front of a dingy looking, three-story building. He stopped the car and went inside. Jamisen came around and opened Mr. Estes' door. "Should we carry him in?"

"I don't know if we should move him or not," Clip answered.

In less than a minute, the driver came back leading a woman dressed in blue and a man dressed in a white coat, who was obviously a doctor. The driver said something to the doctor and pointed to Mr. Estes in the back of the car. The doctor only glanced at Jamisen and Clip before leaning in the car to examine Mr. Estes. He felt for a pulse, and satisfied he was still alive, he took out a small light and shined it in Mr. Estes' eyes, as he raised the lids with his fingers. He then backed back out of the car and said something to the woman, who ran quickly back inside to what Clip and Jamisen decided, must be the hospital.

She returned in less than a minute with another woman pushing a gurney. The doctor pointed at Jamisen, Clip, and the driver and instructed them to load Mr. Estes onto it. It was difficult to get his limp body out of the car, even for two fairly strong boys like Jamisen and Clip. They finally managed to lift him onto the gurney, and the two women pushed him into the hospital.

Clip thought it was dark for a hospital, and the halls looked much dirtier than most public buildings in America—much less a hospital. They pushed Mr. Estes down one hall and then another. The doctor was walking ahead at a fast pace. He opened a door to one of the rooms, and the two women wheeled the gurney in there.

There was very little medical equipment in the room, and everything that was in there looked very old. There was an ancient looking heart monitor and a free standing oxygen tank with a hose and mask attached to it. They helped the two nurses move Mr. Estes to the bed. The doctor immediately put the oxygen mask on him and turned on the tank. A faint whistling sound could be heard as the oxygen escaped the mask.

The doctor unbuttoned Mr. Estes' shirt and used a stethoscope to listen to his heart. He said something to the nurses, and they left the room. In a moment, one of them returned to the room with an I.V. line and bag of clear liquid. Clip assumed it was probably saline. The nurse started the I.V. in Mr. Estes' arm and began the saline drip. A few moments later the other nurse returned to the room with a syringe and a vial of medicine. The doctor took them and drew the syringe halfway full of the medicine, then he injected the contents into the I.V. line.

The doctor listened to his chest once more, and then motioned for Jamisen and Clip to follow him out into the hall.

"Your friend very sick," the doctor said.

"You speak English," said Clip thankful for this small blessing.

"Yes."

"What is the matter with him? Why is he sick?"

"His heart is bad. I think he have heart problem."

"Will he be O.K.?"

"I am sorry. I think not. He is old."

The news hit Clip like a hammer. He slumped down in his chair, uncomprehending to the conversation Jamisen and the doctor continued to have. The doctor left and walked down the dim hall. Just then the taxi driver rounded the corner carrying all three of their backpacks. Jamisen and Clip had completely forgotten about their things. They could have very easily lost that which Mr. Estes had sacrificed his body.

The driver stopped the doctor and conversed with him for a few moments. He then brought the bags to the boys, and laid them at their feet. He pointed at the door to the room. "Sorry," he said. He looked like he wanted to say more but did not know how. He turned to leave and then it hit Jamisen. "Your fare!"

The driver turned back around uncomprehending. Jamisen rummaged in his bag and produced the wad of Yuan he had taken from one of the backpacks. He reached out to hand it to the driver. It was more than what he normally made in a month, but he shook his head and said something in Chinese. Jamisen could not understand him, but he obviously did not want to take the money.

"Please," said Jamisen. "Please, take the money. You have been very kind to us."

The driver still shook his head and smiled, but Jamisen grabbed his hand and forced the wad of bills into it. "Thank you," Jamisen said, giving the man a bow of his head.

The man smiled warmly. "O.K," he said and left.

Clip felt mentally and physically exhausted. "Now what?" he asked Jamisen.

"I guess all we can do is wait . . . and pray."

Clip leaned over with his hands between his knees and began to pray silently. Jamisen got out of his chair and knelt down with his head against the wall. Clip could hear him whispering his prayer softly. Clip tried to concentrate and pray for Mr. Estes' recovery, but his mind began to wander to the events of his life that Mr. Estes was a part of, including this trip.

Clip jerked up just as he was about to fall forward out of the chair. He had drifted to sleep. He looked over at Jamisen, who was still kneeling and praying audibly. A rush of guilt swept over him. What kind of person was he if he couldn't even stay awake to pray for one of his best friends? He bent his head again and pleaded with God to touch Mr. Estes and heal him. Clip reminded God what a faithful servant Mr. Estes had been, and that he had fallen sick doing His work and furthering His Kingdom.

Almost a half hour had passed, and both boys were still praying. One of the nurses came out of the room and went down the hall in the direction the doctor had gone. In a moment, she came back with him. He said nothing to the boys as he walked by and entered the room.

In a few minutes, he came back out and put his hand on Clip's shoulder. "I am sorry. Your friend now dead."

Clip had no response other than to bury his face in his hands and cry. He kept thinking over and over in his mind: "Why? Why?"

Jamisen put his arm around his shoulders and tried to comfort him, but Clip was withdrawn into a world of internal fury. He was mad at himself for not doing more; mad at the Sorlenni, Bell, and the rest for their part; but especially he was mad a God. "How could He let him die? He was a faithful servant?" These words kept rolling over and over in his mind. "Where was the power of prayer when we needed it!?" Clip thought ruefully.

After several minutes, Clip's sobs subsided. "What do we do now?" he asked Jamisen wiping his eyes. "What do we do with his body? How do we get back to England or wherever we are going? Most of the money, the credit cards, and traveler's checks were in Mr. Estes' briefcase."

"I suppose we need to call Brother Lohn."

"What can he do, though? I'm sure he doesn't have enough money to wire to us to fly home and to get Mr. Estes home, and what about our passports? By the time we can get new ones, I can guarantee that Sorlenni will be looking for our names leaving the country."

"Still, we need to call and tell him the situation."

"You're right. I wonder where a phone is around here?" Clip asked in a hoarse whisper.

It was then that they saw the doctor standing patiently

a little way down the hall. He was giving the boys a chance to grieve privately.

Jamisen and Clip both rose and walked to the doctor. "Can we use the telephone?" Clip asked.

"Phone? Yes, come this way."

They followed him to a tiny office that had a desk that was cluttered with medical charts. The walls were lined with bookshelves containing medical journals. The doctor pulled out the chair behind the desk and motioned for Clip to sit down.

"You had better call," he told Jamisen.

Jamisen sat down in a chair in the corner of the office, and the doctor handed him the phone. It was an old, black rotary job that looked like it was from the fifties.

"O.K.?" the doctor asked.

"Yes, thank you," answered Jamisen.

The doctor left and shut the door behind him. Jamisen tried calling Lohn's room first, but there was no answer. It was around noon at Stansberry, so Jamisen had doubted he would be there anyway. He then called the front office at the abbey. It took several minutes for them to locate Lohn, and Jamisen wondered if the doctor would get into trouble for the phone bill.

Lohn finally picked up the phone, and when he found it was Jamisen, he told him to call him back in his room in a minute. Jamisen called collect this time, and Lohn accepted the charges.

"Is Ralph getting too stingy to pay for phone calls now?" he said with a chuckle.

"He's dead, Brother Lohn."

"What?"

"Mr. Estes is dead. We are at a hospital in Xi'an. He died a little while ago from a heart problem."

"God in Heaven, help us. Where is Clip?"

"He is here. We are both fine, but we ran into some trouble."

Jamisen launched into the events that had taken place

since they last talked to Lohn on the phone. It took him a while, and now Clip was thinking about the phone bill. It seemed odd to Clip that he would think about something so trivial at a time like this, but he could not get it out of his head. Actually, when Clip thought about it, everything seemed odd: sitting in a hospital in China, Mr. Estes just dying, being on an expedition to recover ancient scrolls of power. He felt like he was part of some fantasy life that occurred in dreams. "Or nightmares," he thought cynically.

When Jamisen finished telling Lohn all that had happened, there was silence on the other end of the phone. "Brother Lohn?"

"Yes, I am here Jamisen. I'm just trying to figure out what to do. I can come up with money to wire to you somehow, but the passports are a problem. You will have to go to the American embassy and the British embassy for those."

Clip was sitting on the edge of the desk and could hear what Lohn was saying. "Tell him my parents can send us the money, but once they hear Mr. Estes is dead, it's over for me. I'll have to return home. I could never get them to understand the scrolls over the phone. I don't even know if I could in person. But that still doesn't solve the problem of Sorlenni. If he discovers us, he'll follow us and take the scrolls by force, and I don't think Bell will be too nice to us either if he sees us again."

"Clip says that . . ."

"Yes, I heard him. Give me some time to come up with something. Is there a number there where I can reach you?"

"I don't know it."

"Very well. You call me back in an hour."

"O.K. Goodbye."

"God be with you my son. Good bye."

"Well, we are up the creek without a paddle," said Clip.

"How much money do you have? Enough to get us a train ticket to whatever city the embassies are in?"

Clip pulled out his billfold. "Let me see." He opened it

up and was about to count his money when it hit him. "Wait a minute. I may know where we can get help." He dug in one of the small pockets of the billfold that was supposed to hold credit cards and pulled out a business card that said: Mark Stone, Attorney at Law.

"What's that?" asked Jamisen.

"Mr. Estes gave this to me right after we left America. He said if I was in trouble, and he wasn't around, to call this guy. Mr. Estes said that they had been friends for a long time. I would definitely call this trouble, so I'm going to call him."

Clip swapped places with Jamisen and made a collect call to the office number first. When the automated operated asked for his name, he said "Ralph Estes." A secretary answered and accepted the call.

"Just a moment, Mr. Estes, and I'll put you through to Mr. Stone."

Clip waited for a minute on the line then heard, "Ralph! Sorry it took me so long. I had to usher some clients out. What's up?"

"Uhh . . . Mr. Stone, this is Clip Tarence, a friend of Mr. Estes.' He gave me a card with your name on it and said if I was ever in trouble to call you."

"Clip! Hey, I've heard a lot about you. What's the problem?"

"Well, Mr. Stone . . . ," Clip started tearing up. " . . . Mr. Estes is dead."

There was silence on the other end of the line. "Mr. Stone?"

"Yes, I'm sorry, Clip. It just caught me a little off guard. How did it happen?"

"Do you know where we are, Mr. Stone?"

"No. I knew Ralph was returning to England, but then he said he was going to do some traveling with you."

"Do you know why we are traveling around?"

"No, but I figured it had to do with his study. He was

always researching things, but what happened? Where are you now?"

"How long have you known Mr. Estes?"

"He and my father were best friends until my father died several years ago. I have handled his business affairs since I started my practice twenty-years ago, though I've rarely got to see him face-to-face the past ten years since he spent so much time overseas. Is there something I should know? You can trust me to help you."

"Are you a Christian, Mr. Stone?"

"Yes, I am, Clip."

"Well, I really don't have a choice, but I do feel like I can trust you, so I'll start from the beginning. Then I'll leave it for you to decide what to do."

So Clip told Stone everything: the scrolls, the encounter with the bishop and his men, the trip to the hospital. "You can keep the secret or not, Mr. Stone, if you even believe me. But there's no question Jamisen and I are up against it, and we don't know where to turn."

Stone was silent for some time. "I do believe you, Clip. I had great faith in Mr. Estes, and if he had faith in you, that's good enough for me. I can give you my word that I won't divulge your secret unless it becomes absolutely necessary. The first thing we need to do is get you out of the country."

"What about Mr. Estes' body?"

"I'll take care of that, too. Get me the name of the hospital and the phone number. Then you and Jamisen go to a hotel and call me back on my cell? Do you have the number?"

"Yes, it's on the card?"

"Good. I'm going to work everything out, Clip. You've just got to trust me for a little while."

"O.K. Thanks."

"Don't worry. I'm going to get you guys, and what you have, out of there without anybody knowing about it. Now see if you can get me the hospital information."

Jamisen went down the hall and found the doctor working on some medical charts. He took him back to the office and he wrote down the name of the hospital, the phone number to the main office, and the address. Clip read it back to Stone, who instructed them again to go to a hotel.

"We need to call Lohn and tell him that we've got some help now," said Clip after hung up with Stone.

Jamisen called Lohn and explained about their conversation with Stone. Lohn said to keep him posted on what their plans were, and that he would be praying for them.

"Someone is going to call the hospital about arrangements for our friend," said Clip to the doctor. "We are going to a hotel. Thank you very much for all you have done for us."

They visited the bedside of Mr. Estes before they left. His facial features looked serene and content. Both boys cried, and they said their goodbyes.

The doctor was waiting in the hall for them. "Again, I am sorry for your friend. You go to hotel and rest. You two look very bad," he said in jest and patted them on the shoulders. The boys grinned and were appreciative of the doctor's efforts to comfort them.

The doctor called a taxi, and then he walked them to the entrance to wait on it to arrive. When it pulled in a few minutes later, they thanked him again. He told the driver to take them to a hotel.

The taxi pulled away, and the feelings of loss hit Clip once more. He began to cry and to question again the fairness of Mr. Estes' death.

Chapter 14

The taxi took them to a nice hotel. It was actually the nicest one they had seen since arriving in China. Jamisen paid off the clerk with a U.S. twenty and checked them in under a fake name as he had seen Mr. Estes do at the other hotel.

When they got to their room, they immediately called Stone on his cell phone. Clip gave him the number to their room. "You boys get some rest, and I'll call you tonight, which will be morning your time."

"O.K. Thanks Mr. Stone."

"You can call me, Mark."

"Did Mr. Estes?"

"Not since I became his lawyer."

"Then I don't either."

"I can see why he picked you to go with him, Clip. You're a fine young man. Now get some sleep. I'll be in touch."

Clip hung up the phone. "Well, Mr. Stone said he would take care of everything." He flopped in an overstuffed chair and stared at the floor.

"What about the scroll?" asked Jamisen.

"To be honest, I had forgotten about it," Clip said.

Jamisen opened Mr. Estes' pack and removed the plastic bag that contained the scroll. Carefully, he laid it on the small table in the room. Clip scooted to the edge of his seat and inspected the scroll. "It looks pretty ordinary to me," he said. "Old, but ordinary."

The wax seal had broken a little at the edges during the trip from the forest, but other than that, it was in fine shape. "I suppose we need to find a better case to carry it in," Jamisen said looking around the room.

"Here. I've got something," Clip said as he prowled through his backpack. He produced a shaving kit bag with his toiletry items and dumped the contents into the plastic bag that had held the scroll. He then put the scroll in the shaving kit bag. It was almost a perfect fit.

"Are you hungry," Clip asked.

"Famished."

"What do you say we head down to the hotel restaurant and see if we can get something?"

"Do you think they are open this late?"

"Yeah, I saw some people in there when we checked in."

They shouldered their packs and went down to the restaurant and found there was a midnight buffet. This pleased them greatly, for they didn't know how they were going to order. After stuffing themselves, they returned to the room to sleep.

The room was nice, and they each had a queen size bed. To Jamisen, who had never camped before, this was the best aspect of the room other than the shower.

They had just turned the lights off, and it had been quiet for a minute when Jamisen said, "I'm really sorry about Mr. Estes. I know he was a good friend of yours."

Clip wanted to say, he was sorry, too, and that it wasn't fair that God would let a man like Mr. Estes die, especially at such an important time. But he kept the inner turmoil he was feeling suppressed and simply said, "Thanks." They spoke no more, and both of them drifted off to sleep after a time of contemplation.

Stone woke them with a call at midmorning. "Hello, Clip. I have taken care of the arrangements for Mr. Estes' body. I've also got someone coming to help get you out of the country. His name is Kevin Smith, and he should be at your hotel by the afternoon."

"Where's he coming from?"

"He works out of the U.S. embassy in Beijing."

"Does he work for the U.S. government?"

"Not officially. You know those men you said worked for the bishop?"

"Yeah."

"Well, he's like them, except he works for the good guys. He's a friend of a friend, and we can trust him. Plus, time is of the essence, and he's the closest contact to you I have."

"We appreciate all your help, Mr. Stone."

"It's nothing, Clip. You guys are the ones on the front line, not me. Do you know where you want to go when you leave China?"

"England. We need to see Lohn."

"I figure you'd say that. Kevin will get you to London, and I'm going to meet you there. I have some things I need to go over with you."

"How will we know who this Kevin guy is?"

"My friend said he's tall, with blond hair, and he speaks Chinese fluently."

"What about money to pay for our tickets?"

"Don't worry about that. It will be taken care of. Let me know when you will be arriving in London."

"O.K. Thanks again."

Clip explained to Jamisen all that Stone had said to him. It was only an hour before noon, and they had not had any breakfast. They showered and shaved, and then they went down to have brunch in the hotel lobby. After eating, they came back to the room and flipped through the channels on the TV.

"What do you think will happen when we read the scroll?" Jamisen asked.

"I don't know. I guess it depends on what is written on it."

"Have you ever wondered whether we were the ones who were meant to find them?"

"Yeah, I've thought about it, but even if we were not the ones, the *time* we live in is surely right. No one believes in miracles anymore. And there haven't been any big recorded miracles since the time of the Bible. Of course, I can see why people have a hard time believing in miracles these days." Clip muttered the last part with a touch of disgust in his voice.

"What is that supposed to mean?"

Clip was tired of pretending to himself and to Jamisen he was alright with Mr. Estes' death, so he let it all out. "It means, I prayed for Mr. Estes to live when we were sitting out in the hallway of that hospital, and he died within minutes of my prayer. If God won't save a man like Mr. Estes, who was trying to serve Him, then what kind of miracles is He going to perform for a world that lacks a tenth of the faith Mr. Estes had?"

The tears starting welling in Clip's eyes. He did not cry though. He just stared straight ahead, and they ran silently down his face.

"I really don't know what to say to comfort you, other than we never know the will of God."

"So you think it was the will of God for Mr. Estes to die!?"

"Maybe. Or maybe he chose not to intervene. I don't know. No one knows the mind of God. That's what sets Him above us. If we knew His mind, we would be god's ourselves, and that can never be."

"I've heard all the cliché lines like that before, but I never knew how hollow they sounded, until now."

"I agree. They are hollow without faith. Faith is what keeps us in the game, even when the score is against us."

"What about Jesus saying a person could move mountains if you asked in faith? I prayed, and I didn't move a mountain. He died."

"I prayed, too. But maybe it was not a mountain that God wanted moved."

"If my important prayers like that are never answered, how can I have faith?"

"Albert Simpson once said that: 'The time to trust is

when all else fails,' and that 'you will yet thank God for the school of sorrow which was to you the school of faith.' I know I don't have an answer to ease your pain, but the best example I can think of is your childhood. When you were young, did you always understand everything your parents did when rearing you, like bedtimes and doctor visits?"

"No, I guess not."

"Did you ever doubt they loved you, even when you didn't understand why they made you eat right and do this or that?"

"No, I always knew they loved me."

"I know it's a simplistic way to look at it, but that's the way it is with God. We are his children, and we will never fully understand everything he puts in our path, especially the things we don't like."

Clip said no more. He got up and told Jamisen he was going to stretch his legs in the hall. He left the room and walked down the empty hall, past the elevators, and to a large window that overlooked the city. Clip stood there gazing out, with his hands in his pockets. In a barely audible whisper he said, "Lord, I don't know what to think or feel. All I know is that I'm floundering. I want to be steadfast and faithful, but I don't have it in me to do it on my own. Help me Lord. Strengthen me and instill in me the faith to know You are in control, and that You will be there to lift me up when life doesn't go the way I plan. Thank you for Jamisen and his words of encouragement. Take me now and use me please, Lord. In Jesus' name I pray, amen."

Clip returned to the room and found Jamisen still flipping through the channels. "Thanks."

"No problem. I say we take a nap while we are waiting on this Kevin Smith chap. I don't think I can watch another one of these Chinese soap operas."

"Good idea."

Clip was more tired than he thought, for when the phone rang, he looked at the clock and they had been asleep for almost four hours. "Hello?"

"Clip Tarence?"

"Yes."

"This is Kevin Smith. I'm down in the hotel lobby."

"Oh. O.K. Come on up. We're in room 618."

"Be right there."

"Who was that?" asked Jamisen rubbing his eyes.

"It was Kevin Smith. He called from the lobby. He's on his way up."

In a few minutes, there was a knock at the door Clip looked out the peep hole and saw a tall, blond haired man in casual clothes holding a small carry-on bag. Clip opened the door. "Hello. Are you Clip?" Smith said as he offered his hand.

"Yes, sir." Clip shook his hand firmly and invited him in the room.

"And you must be Jamisen," he said shaking Jamisen's hand. "Well, men. I hear you are in a bit of a fix. You must have some friends in high places for some of the strings that are being pulled for you."

"We really appreciate you helping us," said Clip.

"It's no problem. I'm returning a few favors." Even though Smith said this like it was compulsory that he be there, Jamisen and Clip got the impression he would have helped them anyway, without any people calling in any favors.

"Now, as I understand it, you need out of the country fast because there are some not so nice men after you because you've got something they want."

"Yes..." Clip looked like he was going to try and explain what they wanted, but Smith cut him off short.

"I don't need or want to know what you have. My job is to get you out of the country as quick as possible. Mark Stone said you wanted to go to London, so I've got you booked on a flight out of Xi'an at eight o'clock tonight."

Smith unzipped his bag and produced two passports. "Stone also said you needed these." They were U.S. passports, and they had names in them that the boys did not know. They both had several entry and exit stamps from other countries. The only thing that was missing was their pictures.

"Where did you get these?" asked Jamisen.

"I have a friend who works at the embassy. I could only get two U.S. passports on such short notice, so you will have to wing an accent, Jamisen. The fake names are so that you can't be tracked leaving the country or entering England. All we need to do now is add your pictures to them."

Smith pulled a small digital camera from his bag and what looked like a tiny printer. "Alright, stand in front of that wall over there. The white background will be perfect."

Clip stood in front of the wall, and Smith snapped his picture. Jamisen followed suit, and then Smith connected the camera to the printer with a short wire. The printer produced a picture on paper about the size of a business card. Smith then took a razor blade and cut out the pictures. He glued them into the passport using a small bottle of superglue he also had in his bag. After gluing the picture on, he took a piece of clear, sticky plastic and covered the page where he had just glued the picture.

"Done. You are all set Mr. Harper and Mr. Caldwell."

"And these will work?" asked Clip.

"Without a hitch. Now, we've got a couple hours before you have to go to the airport, so what say we go down to the hotel restaurant and get something to eat."

"Sounds good to me. It has become our favorite restaurant in town," Clip said with a grin.

Before heading down, they called Lohn and told him of their plan. They promised to call him when they got to London. They also called Stone on his mobile phone. He was at the airport and booked on a flight to London. He told them the name of a hotel where they could meet. "There will be two rooms reserved under my name. I should get there before you, so just call me from the desk."

Having informed everyone of their itinerary, they went

down to the restaurant. Smith was fluent in Chinese, and he ordered some of the best food the boys had eaten since they arrived in China. They took their time and talked about inconsequential things. He did not ask about why they were in China, and they did not ask about what he did for a living. They knew he worked at the embassy, but they had a feeling it was something more than just processing visa's and passports. They talked mostly about where they were from and Clip and Jamisen's future plans.

As usual, they had brought their bags with them, so they checked out after leaving the restaurant. Smith walked them outside and hailed a taxi for them. He handed Clip a piece of paper and said, "Here's the airline and gate you will be departing from. The tickets were booked as e-tickets under the names on your passports, so just present them at the ticket counter."

Clip and Jamisen had figured that Smith was going to go with them to the airport and see them on the plane, but it looked like he was not.

"We really appreciate all your help. I don't know what we would have done," Clip said shaking his hand.

"Yeah, we owe you one, so if you are ever stranded in England, with bad guys pursuing you, feel free to call me," said Jamisen laughing as he also shook hands with him.

"Hey, that reminds me," said Smith reaching into his pocket. He produced two business cards with his name and phone number. "This is my mobile number. If you are ever in China again and find yourself in a jam, give me a call."

They thanked him again and said goodbye. The taxi ride took almost an hour because the airport was on the far northeast side of the city. The driver dropped them off in front of the entrance, and the two friends entered and started trying to sift through the signs to find the direction they were supposed to go. The main plaza was bustling with people hurrying here and there dragging mounds of luggage or children, and sometimes children on luggage. There were many nationalities to be seen, and Jamisen and Clip blended in with the hodge-podge of travelers.

"There," said Jamisen pointing. "Down at the end is our airline check-in desk."

They started making their way through the crowd of people, when Clip felt a slight tug on his backpack. He half turned, and the next thing he knew, Rollins was chest to chest with him. Clip felt a sharp pain in his side and looked down to see the black steel of a semiautomatic pistol in his rib cage.

Rollins had Clip by the arm keeping him pulled close to him. "Hey, buddy. I hoped I might bump into you."

Jamisen whirled around and started to push Rollins away. "Jamisen, he's got a gun!"

Jamisen pulled up short. "Quiet, or everybody in here is going to know I've got a gun when I blow one of your ribs out your back."

He slipped the hand holding the gun in the pocket of the windbreaker he was wearing, but he kept a hold on Clip's backpack with the other one. "O.K., boys. We're going to go for a little walk. I'll guide you along, Tarence, and you walk right beside me, monk. If you try any thing with me, I have no conscience whatsoever about killing both of you in front of everybody here. You follow directions, and you can still come out of this alive."

He pushed Clip forward and guided him through the mass of people to the far end of the plaza. He then directed them to go through a service door that led into a long hallway with many doors on both sides of the hall. Rollins then told them to walk to the end of the hall and then take a side door that led outside. They found themselves in an alleyway that divided storage garages on either side. The far end of the alley was fenced off, and they could hear cars zooming on the other side. Clip figured they were near the passenger drop off road on which they had just arrived.

Rollins pushed them ahead roughly, now that there

wasn't anyone around. The buildings looked practically abandoned. As they walked down the alley, Clip could see that some of the large, metal doors of the garages were open revealing old airplane parts and broken down service vehicles. Rollins now had his gun out of his pocket and used it to motion them into one of the open garages. They walked over and around old, worn out landing gear tires. There was a small room in the back of the garage that was empty except for an old, broken cigarette vending machine. Rollins pushed Jamisen and Clip in the room, and he followed behind. There was no door, but they were concealed from the alleyway, nonetheless. It was apparent no one was in this area often, so Jamisen and Clip figured it was up to them to save themselves.

"Not too smart leaving your briefcase in the woods, boys."

At these words, Clip's heart sank. So they did have the briefcase.

"How were you expecting to get out of the country without your passports? I would also like to know where your old friend is. I did not see him enter the airport."

Neither Jamisen nor Clip answered him. Rollins raised the gun to chest level. "I suggest you start talking before I lose my patience.

"He's dead," Clip said in a matter-of-fact tone.

"I don't believe you."

"Believe what you want. I don't care. He died in the hospital the night we left you in the woods."

At these words, a flicker of remembrance crossed Rollin's face, and it was not a happy look. "Oh, yes. You had a fun little time leaving us in the woods like that. Well, it doesn't matter about the old man. We've got all the other exits from the city covered. Now all that's left is to see if you've got the scroll or if he took it. Take off your packs and dump them out."

The boys complied, and made a pile of their belongings on the floor. "Now, hold up each thing one at a time and show it to me, then throw it over there," he said point to the floor at his right.

They began holding up each item for his inspection, until he was satisfied the scroll was not hidden in it somewhere. Clip thought about trying to kick the shaving kit bag out of the pile, but there was no where to hide it in the empty room. He decided not to wait until the last to show the bag, so it would not look so obvious. Rollins told him to open it, however, and the scroll was revealed.

"Well, well. You know. I actually believe that the old man is dead. I figured he wouldn't trust you two kids with the scroll and was long gone on a train out of the city. We knew you guys couldn't get passports that quick, but I was ordered to watch the airport anyway. Looks like I drew the right assignment."

Rollins put the scroll in his jacket pocket. "Now all that's left is to make sure there are no loose ends." He raised the gun to Clip's head.

"Hey! You said 'If we cooperate, we would get out of this alive!' said Jamisen in a frightened tone. The realization that they were they were both staring death in the face turned their blood to ice.

"I said you *might* get out of this alive," said Rollins laughing. "I might have had a little more compassion, if I had not had to walk naked out of a forest."

"People will hear," said Clip frantically trying to find a way to talk their way out of being shot.

"Not with all that traffic out there."

Clip had made up his mind to rush him and hoped he or Jamisen one could get the gun away before they were shot, when suddenly and arm appeared through the doorway leveling a small semiautomatic pistol at Rollin's head. "Throw the gun down," said a familiar voice. Into the room stepped Smith.

Rollin's was caught so off guard he did not comply at first. "I promise I will not tell you again," said Smith in a voice as cold as steel.

Rollins quickly threw the gun down with a clank on the floor. "Now, put your hands on your head and step against the wall face forward." Smith patted him down, until he was satisfied he had no more weapons.

"My gosh, it's good to see you, Mr. Smith!" said Clip in between breaths of relief.

"How did you get here or even know to get here?" asked Jamisen.

"I've been following you since you left the hotel. I wanted to make sure that you got off O.K., and it would be easier to help if no one knew I was with you, which turned out to be a good thing. Now, Mr. . . . ?"

"Rollins," Clip offered.

"Mr. Rollins, lay face down on the ground," Smith instructed. When he was down, Smith placed his knee in his back and let his full weight down on him. "You boys probably need to get your stuff and go into the next room for this."

At these words, Rollins tried to roll out from under Smith, but Smith rammed the barrel of the pistol hard into his temple and cocked the hammer. This stopped Rollin's squirming.

"What are you going to do?" asked Clip.

"The same thing he was going to do to you," answered Smith in a nonchalant voice.

"I wasn't going to kill them! I was just messing with them!"

"Shut up!" Smith said as he rammed the gun into the side of his head again.

Jamisen and Clip gathered up their belongings from the floor, and Jamisen removed the scroll from Rollin's jacket. If Smith showed any interest in the scroll, he hid it well.

They started to leave the room, when Jamisen turned back and said, "You mustn't kill him."

"What? Why?"

"He's right," Clip said. "You shouldn't kill him."

"Look, I know you boys don't have any experience in

this, but I do. Let me assure you that his guy was ten seconds away from blowing off both your heads, and he would have slept like a baby tonight. If we let him go, I promise he will try to blow your head off again if he gets the chance."

"That's just it," said Jamisen. "It would make us no better than him."

"Let it rest on my conscience, not yours."

"If we could have prevented it, it will be on my conscience," answered Jamisen.

"What if we tie him up real good, and leave him in here. He might go days before anyone will find him, and we will be long gone to France by then," offered Clip.

Smith stared at the back of Rollin's head for a minute, then he whispered into his ear, "I guess this is your lucky day, but if I ever see you again, I can promise I want be quite as forgiving as these boys were. Do you understand me?" He asked this last part as he turned the barrel of the gun sharply in the side of his head.

"Yeah," Rollins grunted.

"O.K., boys. See if you can find something in there to tie him up with."

Jamisen and Clip searched the outer part of the garage and found some oily rope that was being used to tie several of the old tires in a bundle. They gave the rope to Smith, who expertly tied Rollin's hands behind his back, and then he bent his feet back nearly to his hips, where he then tied his ankle to his wrists. Using an old rag, he made a gag that he tied around Rollin's mouth and head. Rollins looked like a pig ready to be put on a spit.

"Well, that should do it. I personally hope it takes more than a few days for somebody to find him and all that's left is a shirt full of bones," Smith said grimly.

"Thank you," said Jamisen.

"I hope you boys know, that sometimes the nicer you treat the world, the worse the world treats you. But . . . I guess the world could use more people like you and less people like me."

They left Rollins to his fate and made their way back to the airport terminal. Smith hid his gun in a restroom for later retrieval and escorted Jamisen and Clip to their departure gate.

When boarding for the plane began, they said their goodbyes. "We really owe you a big one," said Clip.

"Nah. It was a pleasure to help you out. I don't know what you guys are a part of, but I think you are on your way to making a difference, and I think you will do a fine job. Be sure and look me up, if you are ever back in China."

They promised to do that as they shook his hand one last time. Smith stayed at the gate until the plane pulled away. Jamisen and Clip could barely see him from the window of the plane, and they discussed the many helpful people God had placed in their path.

Chapter 15

For the first time in many days, the boys felt safe and free. "That was a smart little detail you added back at the airport, saying that we were headed to France. Maybe that will throw them off our trail for a while, if Rollins gets loose."

"It probably won't work long. They know you are from the abbey and about Lohn, and it won't take them long to figure out about me if they've got my passport. We are going to have to figure out what we are going to do next. What do you think Lohn will want to do about the other two scrolls?"

"I don't know, but I don't think we should return to the abbey. When we call Lohn from London, we need to decide on a place to meet."

"Surely he will be for finding the other scrolls."

"I hope so, but he may think it is too dangerous, and he has the directions."

"Yeah, but Mr. Estes died trying to recover the scrolls. If nothing else, we owe it to him to find the others before Sorlenni does. We now know he's got the briefcase. It will just depend on how fast they can get past the security on the laptop as to when they will try to find them. We've got to beat them to the punch."

"You don't have to convince me. I agree with you. But on the other hand, do you see Lohn turning two eighteen-year-old kids loose to trot across the world on a scavenger hunt, with men hunting us down, ready to kill us?"

"Lohn could come with us," Clip offered.

"I hate to be morbid, but what if something happened to all three of us? Then who would be left to carry on the search for the scrolls?"

The boys batted options like this around, until their in-flight meal arrived. After they ate, both boys decided some much-needed rest was in order, so they slept the rest of the flight to London.

Upon arriving in London, they were both a little worried about their fake passports once again. Images of being detained and having their belongings confiscated flashed in their minds, but they passed through with no problems. They caught a taxi outside the airport, and rode to the hotel where Stone said he had them a room.

The hotel Stone had picked was the the nicest hotel Jamisen or Clip had ever seen. The lobby looked like a Victorian explosion of crystal and marble. Dozens of large chandeliers hung from the ceiling, countless statues and vases adorned the walls and corners of the huge room. There were plush sofas with gold trim and tasseled pillows, and antique wicker chairs and coffee tables filled the center of the room, with servants on hand to serve tea.

They went to the desk and asked them to ring Stone's room on the house phone. "Hello, Clip. I'm glad you made it O.K. Kevin Smith called me after he saw you off and told me what happened. That was a close call. You boys come on up. I'm in room 409. Your room is right beside mine. It's in my name, so I've got your keys."

They went up to meet their benefactor in person for the first time. They knocked on the door and were greeted by a bear of a man. Stone was well over six feet tall and had a large barrel chest and broad shoulders. It was obvious he had once had a muscular physique, even though his belly protruded out of the Polo shirt he was wearing. He offered Jamisen and Clip and big, meaty paw which he used to shake their hands with great, bone crushing enthusiasm. "Come in. Come in."

Jamisen and Clip entered the room massaging their numb hands. "It's great to finally meet you boys in the flesh."

"We want to thank you for all your help, Mr. Stone," said

Clip. "I guess we would still be stuck in China if it wasn't for you, and maybe worse."

"It was nothing. I'm just glad you boys made it safe and sound. That was some crazy business at the airport. It was lucky Smith was there to help. I guess he was the right man for the job."

"Yeah, we owe him our lives," said Jamisen.

"Have you boys eaten?"

"Not since supper on the plane," answered Clip.

"Well, it's almost supper time here, so why don't we grab a bite, and then we have some things to discuss."

"That sounds great," Clip said, "but we need to call Lohn first and let him know what's going on."

Jamisen called Lohn and told him what had happened at the airport. "I don't think it is safe for you there anymore, Brother Lohn. They know we will probably try to go back there."

"I'm afraid you are right. I suppose I should find some excuse to leave and meet you away from here, but I don't know where we can stay that we cannot be traced."

"I know," said Jamisen. "What about the place you took me to visit once? The place where your friend Brother Aaron is buried?"

"Han Milean?"

"Yes."

"That's a good idea, lad. I will leave today and ready the place. You come when you can."

"Very well. We will meet you there as soon as we can."

When Jamisen got off the phone, he explained to Clip and Stone what had been discussed. "That's a good idea," said Clip, "but how should we get there?"

"We can fly to Leeds and then take a bus to York. From there, we can take another bus to Oswaldkirk. A few miles outside the village is a trail that leads to Han Milean."

"I think that is probably the best plan for now. It's too

easy to track people in the city. We need to regroup and figure out what we are going to do," Clip said.

"I really don't know how to advise you on this, boys. But I do think you need to meet with Lohn and decide your next move," Stone said.

They headed down to yet another hotel restaurant. It was good to be eating Western food again, although it seemed heavier than the food they had been eating for the past week.

Mark Stone turned out to be a jovial man, who could find a joke in almost anything. He told them more about himself and his family. His law practice was in Indianapolis. "You know, Mr. Estes lived in Indianapolis for a long time. It is where the headquarters for his company was. I worked there in the summers. He and my father were good friends. My father owned a shipping company and took care of all Mr. Estes' business."

Stone learned more about Jamisen and Clip, and they went into greater detail concerning their experiences in China. After a good meal and a good conversation, they returned to the room ready to tackle the business Stone wanted to discuss.

He first produced a briefcase and withdrew a folder containing many papers. "I think you better have a seat over here, Clip," Stone said gesturing to a chair beside a small desk. Stone sat across from Clip and placed onto the table the papers from the folder. "Clip, I don't know what else to do but come right out and say it. Mr. Estes left you one million dollars."

Clip sat there stunned. He could not formulate any words to respond to what Stone had just told him.

"He also left you his property and home in Kawana. That's only about ten percent of what he actually had in assets, but he had the rest stipulated for other organizations and charities. Most of the money went to overseas missions."

Clip's mind was racing. He was finally able to say, "Why?"

"He really liked you, Clip, and he placed a lot of faith in you. He didn't have any close family, so you were the natural choice. To be honest with you, I tried to get him to set it up as a trust fund in case you hadn't graduated college when he died. I figured a kid would blow the money and probably never finish school, but Mr. Estes would not hear of it. He said he trusted you beyond a doubt, and that money or not, he knew you would finish school.

"That brings me to the last thing in his will. He also left you one million dollars to give away any way you see fit. The money is in your name, and there is no binding stipulation that would force you to give it away. Again, against my advice, Mr. Estes said he trusted you to do the right thing."

"Why does he want me to give one million dollars away?" Clip asked, still trying to get a handle on the proceedings.

"I asked that same question, and he told me one of the greatest things in life was giving to others and helping those in need. He wanted you to learn that I guess. There is no timetable on when you have to give it away, nor is there an amount stipulation. You can give as much or as little as you want, when you want because technically the money is yours. It was deposited in your account with the other money, so nothing but your conscience could stop you from keeping it. However, after meeting you in person, I don't think Mr. Estes' trust was misplaced.

"Now, I did some fast work and called in a couple of favors to get this quickly for you because I have a feeling you are going to need it if you continue with your search." He handed Clip an envelope, a debit card, and a checkbook. Clip opened the envelope and counted two thousand dollars in cash. He opened the checkbook and it had his name printed on the checks. "Here's your pin number for your debit card. The full two million is in the account at your disposal, minus the two thousand dollars cash I just gave you. It took a lot of finagling to get it done so quickly, but it's there for you to use as you see fit. I think Mr. Estes would want it that way."

"What about Mr. Estes' body?" asked Clip.

"His body is being cremated, and the ashes will be sent

to the U.S. He wanted to be buried at a cemetery near his old home outside of Indianapolis. Any more questions?"

"I really don't know what to say."

"I know, son. It's a big responsibility Mr. Estes has given you, but I think you'll do fine."

Clip had to sign some papers for Stone. They talked some more about Mr. Estes and his wishes, until it grew late. Jamisen and Clip headed to their room to sleep, for they wanted to leave for the bus station early in the morning.

Though they were tired, they stayed up a while talking about what Clip had been given. "You know, I don't feel like a millionaire," Clip said offhandedly.

"No, and you don't look like one either," Jamisen said with a laugh. "What will you do with the million you are supposed to give away?"

"I have no idea. I don't even know what I'm going to do with my million. You know, a year ago I could have made a mile long list of things I wanted to buy if I had even a thousand dollars, but after what we've been through, it all seems so trivial."

"Yeah, I know what you mean."

"To be honest, I don't want to even think about it anymore tonight. It kind of depresses me to know that I got all this money because Mr. Estes died. It wasn't much of a trade off if you ask me."

They turned off the lights and went to bed, but Clip did not stop thinking about it. He lay awake trying to come to grips with what had happened, until a couple hours later he finally drifted off to sleep.

Chapter 16

The boys had an early breakfast with Stone. They told him their plan to travel to Han Milean and decide with Lohn what to do next. Stone walked them out of the hotel, and they said their goodbyes.

"I wish you boys all the luck in the world, and more than that, I will be praying for you."

"Thank you for all your help. We would not have made it without you Mr. Stone," said Clip.

"Yes, you have been a true Godsend, Mr. Stone," affirmed Jamisen.

"You boys take care. I'm sure I'll see you again one day. Hopefully, it will be one day soon. You've got my card if you need me." With that he walked back into the hotel, and the boys hailed a taxi to take them to the bus station.

On the way, they stopped at a bank so that Clip could exchange the money Stone had given him the night before for British pounds, and they made it just in time to catch the early bus to York. The bus made dozens of stops along the way, and they did not arrive in York until the following morning. They then caught a tour bus to Oswaldkirk.

The tiny village was quaint and had a historical mystique about it. The boys ate lunch at a small café and they then bought some food to take with them to Han Milean. They bought bread and cheese and some candy bars, and they also bought a bottle of water for each of them. Jamisen led the way out of town, and they tried to hitch a ride to the trail that led to Han Milean. The few cars that passed them on the old, rarely used road never stopped, and they ended up walking the few miles to the dirt path that led to Han Milean.

The landscape of the Northern Yorkshire Moors was

beautiful to Clip, who loved rural areas. It was a different kind of wilderness than he was used to in Kawana, but it was still beautiful to him with its rolling hills and untamed landscape.

They walked down the trail until they were out of sight of the road and stopped to snack on the candy bars they brought. Clip scanned the horizon and felt transported back to times long gone. He wondered what it must have been like for the peoples who settled this wild land. He knew it was the same kind of people who eventually came to America and settled his town of Kawana.

They were both excited to see Lohn, so they did not rest long. They made it to the hill above Han Milean in less than an hour after their break. They could see a tiny line of smoke coming from the chimney, and they could also see a light in the window.

They strode down the hill with great purpose and speed and arrived at the doorstep slightly out of breath. Jamisen knocked on the door, and it was opened, producing the grinning face of Lohn. "Heaven be praised, and God be glorified. You made it. Come in lads, and let's have a long talk."

They entered the room, and Clip found it to be almost exactly like Mr. Estes had described it to him. It seemed like it was years ago when he was at Mr. Estes' house listening to a fantastic tale of hidden scrolls.

The only noticeable change Jamisen saw since his last visit there was the stacks of nonperishable food stuffs that lined the shelves. Lohn had evidently been busy in preparation for their stay. "It looks like you are stocked for a siege," said Jamisen.

"I didn't know how long we would be here, so I wanted to be prepared. Sit down, and I'll get you something to drink. Then you can tell me everything from the beginning without being hurried."

So they sat down in front of the fireplace, which had only warm coals in it, and began to tell of their trip from the point when they left Stansberry Abbey. Both boys contributed to the tale, one filling in where the other left off. Lohn only interrupted them once to throw some wood on the fire and refill their mugs.

They told of their meeting Abraham and his kindness, of their first night in Xi'an, and of their first visit to Mount Zohngnan. They told of their search of the temple and the discovery Jamisen made and how they had to traverse the forest one marker at a time. They told of their discovery of the cave and the trials they faced in it, and they told of the waiting surprise when they came out with the scroll. They told of their escape and Mr. Estes' death that night. They told of the kind doctor, and they told of Stone and Smith's help. They told of the incident at the airport and their final departure. They told of their meeting with Stone and, and they told about Mr. Estes' will. They finally told of their journey to Han Milean, and by this time it was late in the evening.

Lohn had sat enraptured by their story, only breaking his silence to clarify a point now and then. "You boys have certainly been delivered by the hand of God. We have much to be thankful for, even after the loss of our friend."

Jamisen and Clip agreed wholeheartedly. "God placed the right person at the right time in our path," said Clip.

Now came the part Jamisen and Clip had been eagerly anticipating. "Are you ready to see the scroll?" Clip asked Lohn.

"Yes, please," Lohn answered. His eyes began to dance and anticipation flooded his features.

Clip took the shaving kit bag from his backpack and removed the scroll from it. He handed it to Lohn, who handled it reverently. He held it up close to his eyes for inspection, and he stroked the seal gently.

"What do we do now," asked Jamisen.

Lohn looked at the scroll. "I think we should get a good night's sleep tonight, and then first thing at dawn, we should read the scroll."

That sounded good to the boys. Jamisen and Clip made

pallets in front of the fire from blankets Lohn had brought, while Lohn slept in the room that used to be Aaron's.

The morning came after a fitful night sleep for them all. During the night, they had each contemplated the reading of the scroll and what the ramifications might hold. Bleary eyed, but excited, they ate a hasty breakfast of bread, cheese, and water.

They cleared the table and laid a clean, white cloth on it. Clip then retrieved the scroll and placed it on the cloth. With a sharp knife, Lohn carefully cut the wax seal loose from the parchment. Jamisen and Clip both had goose bumps on their arms as they leaned in close to observe Lohn. After breaking the seal, Lohn started to open the scroll, and then he paused for a moment. "If you boys don't mind, I would like to read this outside."

Jamisen and Clip had no objections, although they did wonder what had given Lohn pause to think. Lohn picked up the scroll, and they followed him outside into the early hours of the morning. The sun had only been up a short while, and the newness of the day could still be felt. Lohn walked to the back of the house, where it became apparent to the boys why he wanted to go outside. He stood beside a simple stone cross that marked the resting place of Aaron.

The boys stood opposite Lohn on the other side of the grave. Lohn stared at the cross and spoke softly. "I wish Ralph could be here with us, old friend. In the end, I think he had more work in it than even you did. I know you both are in a happier place, but we are the worse for it. We honor the work you performed in God's service."

Soft tears fell from Clip's face at the mention of Mr. Estes. Through blurry eyes, he watched as Lohn unrolled the scroll carefully and began to read:

"Lord God, Creator of Heaven and Earth, The Giver of Life and Salvation, The Steadfast Hope, hear the prayer of Your humble servant."

Jamisen and Clip felt more than goose bumps now. The

air around them began to stir, their skin began to tingle, and their hair felt as if it were standing on end. The more Lohn read, the more tangible the words seemed, as if the words had taken form and were passing through them. Their limbs became heavy, and it was a struggle to stand. The wind increased in strength until they had to strain to hear Lohn's words:

"The world of man wavers in its faith, dear God. Sickness, disease, and infirmity are rampant in Your creation, yet man looks to himself for the cure.

"Remind this world who is the Great Healer. Please instill in this cynical world the faith to ask for healing powers much like You granted Elijah and Elisha, and even Your Apostles.

"We are not worthy of Your grace, Lord, but forgive us our rebellious nature. Hear our prayer and answer, Father, in the name of Your Son, Jesus Christ, our Savior and Redeemer."

When Lohn uttered the last syllable, the scroll began to disintegrate and fell apart in his hand then turned to a fine dust that was blown away by the swirling wind. When the last spec was swept away from their vision by the rushing currents, the wind instantly stopped. For a few, brief seconds, all was still and silent as stone. No birds could be heard, no trees creaking, and no insects buzzing. Lohn, Jamisen, and Clip could not move. It was as if the world stood still in deference for this supplication to its Creator.

The stillness lasted only a moment, and all was normal again. The feeling returned to Jamisen and Clip's body. In fact, they felt better than they ever had in their lives. Lohn stood gazing at his hands that once held the scroll. He shook his head, as if waking from a trance and smiled up at the sky.

"Did you feel that?" Jamisen asked them.

"I felt like I was being pressed in on all sides but not in a bad way," Clip answered. "My skin felt like it was going to dance right off my bones, but it didn't hurt. I don't really know how to explain any of it."

"Me either," said Jamisen. "What about you, Brother Lohn?"

Lohn lowered his gaze back down from the blue sky. He seemed like a man contented beyond description. "To be honest with you lads, the last thing I remember is opening the scroll. I can't even tell you what language it was written in. I can hear the words that I read in my mind, as if it was a memory, but I have no recollection of reading them. All I know is that I was staring at the sky, feeling the best in body and spirit that I've felt my whole life. Then I heard you call my name."

Jamisen and Clip described to Lohn what they had seen, felt, and heard. The words poured from their mouths like a fountain, and they felt even better with the telling of the event.

"What do you think it means? The prayer I mean," Clip asked. "All the talk of healing. Who will be healed?"

"I don't know," answered Lohn. "We may never know, but I do believe the power God was called down today."

Jamisen looked at the world around him and sighed. "I'm ashamed to say that my faith was increased today. It's like I experienced something tangible in my relationship with God. I feel guilty because I remember what Jesus said to Thomas, 'Because thou hast seen me, thou hast believed: blessed are they that have not seen, and yet have believed.'"

"You have nothing to feel guilty about, my son," said Lohn laying a comforting hand on his shoulder. "Mark 9:24 also says that Jesus helped the man who said, 'I believe; help thou my unbelief.' You will find that God strengthens our faith by what *He* does for our lives, not what *we* do for Him."

Chapter 17

"I still worry about you, lads," Lohn said for the third time since they started their conversation. They were sitting in front of the hearth discussing what they were to do about the remaining two scrolls. The experience they had that morning was still fresh on their minds, but Jamisen and Clip were advocating leaving as soon as possible to find the other two scrolls.

"We have to assume that Sorlenni will be able to get into Mr. Estes' laptop and have access to the directions. The quicker Jamisen and I leave, the better chance we have of recovering the scrolls before Sorlenni can figure out where they are."

"Yes, but it's not like a church scavenger hunt, Clip. These men will kill you next time if you get in their way. I don't think Ralph would approve of it, and I'm sure your parents would not."

"That's all the more reason we must move quickly," said Jamisen. "We stand a good chance of finding the scrolls before they even understand the directions."

"Look," said Clip leaning forward with an earnest look on his face. "I don't pretend to say that there is no danger involved, and I don't pretend to think Jamisen and I are invincible to all the danger that Sorlenni and the rest of the world has to offer. But I also can't stand by and pretend that I'm helpless to stop Sorlenni from obtaining the scrolls, especially after what I experienced this morning."

"I can see I will get nowhere arguing with you two. If you are determined to go, then I'm coming with you."

Jamisen and Clip exchanged looks. "Clip and I have been discussing it, and we think that is a bad idea. We admit the danger is real, and there is an outside chance that something could happen to us. If it does, someone needs to carry on the task of getting the scrolls, especially if Sorlenni gets them."

"So you lads expect me to just sit here on my hands and wait for you, while you traipse across the globe meeting danger head on? You are daft. We all go, or none goes. Don't you youngsters forget, I have the directions, not you."

Jamisen and Clip relented. In fact, once it was settled, they both felt a little relieved that Lohn would be coming with them. Lohn went to a cabinet and brought out a file that contained many notes and maps. He spread them on the table for the boys to inspect by the light of the oil lamp. They decided which scroll to search for next, and by dawn the next morning, they were on the trail with their backs to Han Milean.

Lohn, Jamisen, and Clip did not see or hear about the impact of the prayer until a few days after the reading. Every news outlet was carrying stories of miraculous healings taking place all over the world.

According to the reports, Christians around the world were healing people of all manner of ailments and sicknesses in the name of God. Men, women, and children were getting up and walking out of hospitals. Terminal patients, who were sent home to die, were out buying groceries or working in the yard. Entire villages in Africa that were ravaged by AIDS were being healed and made new following the prayers of faithful missionaries. Victims of paralysis who were confined to wheelchairs were up and walking. Persons who were blind were given sight to take in the wonder of God's creation. It was a time of intense joy and wonder. The reports were too many and too far-reaching to be coincidence. The attention of the world was turned to the healing power God gave to the body and ultimately to the spirit.

Not everyone who was sick was made well, and not every infirmity was healed. Wherever the hands of the faithful were placed, their prayers were answered, but the pleadings of the lost went unheeded. Charlatans and deceivers arose to steal some of the light, and many tried to use these miracles for personal gain.

The great healing power that was given to the servants of God lasted only a few days. Science tried to explain it away. Politicians, world leaders, and even other religions tried to take credit for it. Many nonbelievers hardened their hearts and drew no closer to accepting the sovereignty of God, but through it all, the world was forced to face the reality of a divine power that intervened in the reviving and saving of life.

Clip looked out of the window of the plane from his seat in first class. Below he could see the blue water glistening from the sun as they approached the Greek Islands. On one of those islands was the second scroll he, Jamisen, and Lohn meant to find, and he could almost feel God's hand pushing him toward it.

Contact author Jared Bigham
or order more copies of this book at

TATE PUBLISHING, LLC

127 East Trade Center Terrace
Mustang, Oklahoma 73064

(888) 361 - 9473

Tate Publishing, LLC

www.tatepublishing.com